Perl 6 Quick Syntax Reference

A Pocket Guide to the Language, the Core Modules, and the Community

J.J. Merelo

Apress®

Perl 6 Quick Syntax Reference: A Pocket Guide to the Language, the Core Modules, and the Community

J.J. Merelo
Granada, Spain

ISBN-13 (pbk): 978-1-4842-4955-0   ISBN-13 (electronic): 978-1-4842-4956-7
https://doi.org/10.1007/978-1-4842-4956-7

Copyright © 2019 by J.J. Merelo

Managing Director, Apress Media LLC: Welmoed Spahr
Acquisitions Editor: Steve Anglin
Development Editor: Matthew Moodie
Coordinating Editor: Mark Powers

Cover designed by eStudioCalamar

Cover image designed by Freepik (www.freepik.com)

Distributed to the book trade worldwide by Springer Science+Business Media New York, 233 Spring Street, 6th Floor, New York, NY 10013. Phone 1-800-SPRINGER, fax (201) 348-4505, e-mail orders-ny@springer-sbm.com, or visit www.springeronline.com. Apress Media, LLC is a California LLC and the sole member (owner) is Springer Science + Business Media Finance Inc (SSBM Finance Inc). SSBM Finance Inc is a **Delaware** corporation.

For information on translations, please e-mail editorial@apress.com; for reprint, paperback, or audio rights, please email bookpermissions@springernature.com.

Apress titles may be purchased in bulk for academic, corporate, or promotional use. eBook versions and licenses are also available for most titles. For more information, reference our Print and eBook Bulk Sales web page at www.apress.com/bulk-sales.

Any source code or other supplementary material referenced by the author in this book is available to readers on GitHub via the book's product page, located at www.apress.com/9781484249550. For more detailed information, please visit www.apress.com/source-code.

Printed on acid-free paper

To my wife, Charo, who makes everything worth the while.

To my daughters, Cecilia, Elena, and Charo, who are the reasons I started learning Perl 6 in the first place.

To the whole Perl 6 community, who are kinda my second family, but very specially to Liz and Wendy, because they have always helped; to Raiph Mellor, who knows everything and helps everyone in Stack Overflow; and of course, to Larry Wall.

Also to cooking a good meal, sleeping a good siesta, and beers with friends and family.

Table of Contents

About the Author

J.J. Merelo is a professor at the University of Granada, where he has been teaching since 1988. He has a PhD in Physics, and he has been using Perl since 1994 and Perl 6 intensively since December 2016. Recently, he has been working on the Perl 6 documentation, and he released a series of Perl 6 modules featuring evolutionary algorithms and Unicode.

He can be followed at `dev.to/JJ`, `github.com/JJ`, and jjmerelo on Twitter and Telegram.

About the Technical Reviewer

 **Massimo Nardone** has more than 24 years of experience in security, web/mobile development, cloud, and IT architecture. His true IT passions are security and Android.

He has been programming and teaching how to program with Android, Perl, PHP, Java, VB, Python, C/C++, and MySQL for more than 20 years.

He holds a Master of Science degree in Computing Science from the University of Salerno, Italy.

He has worked as a Project Manager, Software Engineer, Research Engineer, Chief Security Architect, Information Security Manager, PCI/SCADA Auditor, and Senior Lead IT Security/Cloud/SCADA Architect for many years.

His technical skills include security, Android, cloud, Java, MySQL, Drupal, Cobol, Perl, web and mobile development, MongoDB, D3, Joomla, Couchbase, C/C++, WebGL, Python, Pro Rails, Django CMS, Jekyll, Scratch, etc.

He worked as visiting lecturer and supervisor for exercises at the Networking Laboratory of the Helsinki University of Technology (Aalto University). He holds four international patents in the PKI, SIP, SAML and Proxy areas.

He currently works as the Chief Information Security Officer (CISO) for Cargotec Oyj, and he is member of ISACA Finland Chapter Board.

Massimo reviewed more than 45 IT books for different publishers and he coauthored *Pro JPA in Java EE 8* (Apress, 2018), *Beginning EJB in Java EE 8* (Apress, 2018), and *Pro Android Games* (Apress, 2015).

Acknowledgments

I am very grateful to Moritz Lenz for offering me the opportunity to publish my first *real* book, and of course to Apress and to Mark Powers, Massimo Nardone, and Matthew Moodie, specially Mark, who's supported me through the whole process. Mark has been specially patient with my fumbles through the editorial process and quite supportive through the whole writing process. Of course, I take responsibility for all errors in code or in the text itself.

I needed to ask lots of questions in Stack Overflow to clarify things, because Perl 6 is still a young language and some things need to be clarified. These persons have been very diligent in answering those questions: the aforementioned Liz Mattijsen and Raiph Mellor, but also Håkon Hægland, Jonathan Worthington, Brad Gilbert, Kaiepi (Ben Davies), guifa, Lukas Valle, and some others. You really helped me over the small bumps in the road. And you really help the community by answering What Needs To Be Answered.

The persons in the #perl6 IRC channel have also been helpful and supportive, and they are a great community to belong to. You know what they say: learn the language, stay thanks to the community. Just drop by and say hi, or participate in one of the monthly hackathons, or ask any question you need to be answered Right Now. We'll be there for you.

Which reminds me of *Friends*. It's the best series ever, and watching *Friends* alone or with family never fails to improve my mood. Or, for that matter, provide a (good) reason for procrastinating.

CHAPTER 1

Running Perl 6

How to Install Perl 6 or Simply Have It Ready to Run Your Scripts or Programs

Perl 6 is a programming language, and as such it is a part of a development ecosystem that includes a series of applications. Some of them will be used throughout this book, so here are a few things that you might want to install before you get to Perl 6 itself.

- **Git** is the prime source control and development workflow tool. You might need it to download some Perl 6 modules, or for certain ways of installing it from source.

- **A programming editor**. Perl 6 has its very own integrated development environment (IDE) called Comma, whose license you can acquire from Edument. A community edition was released in March 2019. This IDE includes most of the goodies you could wish for, including syntax highlighting, program running, and documentation preview. Among the rest of the editors, Atom probably has the best support, including highlighting and syntax checking. Other editors, like Emacs, VS Code, and vim, also support Perl 6 and might be enough if you are already familiar with them.

© J.J. Merelo 2019
J.J. Merelo, *Perl 6 Quick Syntax Reference*, https://doi.org/10.1007/978-1-4842-4956-7_1

- **Docker** is a service isolation framework, which is nowadays used widely also for package distribution. Installing it will help you avoid installing things permanently on your system. You can also get particular applications working quickly by just using their name.

- A lot of action in the Perl 6 world happens in **Internet Relay Channels**. Although you can access some of them from the browser, getting your own IRC desktop client will smooth your entrance through seamless authentication and some automation.

You are also going to run some scripts from the command line. Basic understanding of how this works, and how to get to it in different operating systems, always helps. Since you are going to be installing Perl 6 and other things that go along with it, an understanding of packaging systems like apt (the Debian and Ubuntu packaging system, which you will use by default) as well as Chocolatey/NuGet for Windows or Brew for Mac will come in handy.

Once you are ready with this, proceed to installing Perl 6.

Perl 6 on Your Very Own Computer

OK, are you ready? Let's get down to it.

But oh, wait just a minute. You need to know a bit of what Perl 6 is made of to understand what you will actually be installing.

In order to implement a concurrent core and have full support of Unicode, as well as other goodies, Perl 6 runs in a virtual machine designed just for it. This virtual machine is called MoarVM, and it is the one that eventually runs the code that is generated by the programs you write. But this is not the only VM used by Perl 6: the Java virtual machine is also targeted, and in development, although already usable, is a JavaScript VM (that allows it to run Perl 6 on the browser, but more on this later). So, here's the foundation of Perl 6: a virtual machine (to choose among three).

The problem is now you need to generate *native* code for three virtual machines out of high-level Perl 6 code. This might be a problem, since you need to translate every little primitive from Perl 6 to them. This is usually solved using some intermediate language, which in this case is called NQP, or Not Quite Perl. That's the second part.

The third part is the interpreter itself. Perl 6 is a language defined by a set of tests, and any interpreter that passes the tests can be rightfully called Perl 6. For the time being, that's a set of just one member, which is called Rakudo. Rakudo, besides, is written (mostly) in Perl 6. Since Rakudo is written in Perl 6, you need NQP to compile it to native code in the virtual machine you will be using, and you need to have all three parts installed: Rakudo, NQP, and either MoarVM or JVM or the JavaScript virtual machine.

This is what you actually install when you install Perl 6. Let's *now* get down to it.

Your best option to install Perl 6 on any operating system is to use the Rakudo Star (Rakudo∗) distribution. It includes all you need to run a Perl 6 program, plus modules and utilities to install new modules and work comfortably on the command line. There is a new Rakudo Star version every four months: every November, April, and June. It includes self-installing packages for Mac and Windows, and a set of binaries for a generic Linux. This Rakudo∗ will cover most of your needs for Perl 6, since it also packs some modules that make your life easier, like the Linenoise library for command-line editing in the REPL.

However, Perl 6 produces new versions every month. Sometimes, these versions include considerable improvements, and always bug fixes and implementation of new features. There are several ways to install them on your computer:

- Use `rakudobrew`, a version manager, to download, compile, and install the latest version. Once it has been installed, typing

  ```
  rakudobrew list-available
  ```

  will give you a list of versions available for download in the shape `year.month`, for instance, 2018.12 for the version that was published in December 2018. You can install that version via

  ```
  rakudobrew build moar 2018.12
  ```

  which will download and build the stack that starts with MoarVM and that version of Perl 6.

- Use Docker containers, with the added advantage that you don't need any specific tooling, just the Docker client and server. For instance,

  ```
  docker run -it jjmerelo/alpine-perl6:2018.11
  ```

  can be used as a direct substitute for Rakudo version 2018.11. You can also pull the official Rakudo Star containers using `docker pull rakudo-star`. Other Docker containers are available; however, this is the only official one.

- Claudio Ramírez creates, every month, updated packages for many Linux distros for Rakudo. Check the GitHub repo at `https://github.com/nxadm/rakudo.pkg` for instructions on how to download Perl 6 for Debian/Ubuntu, Fedora, and openSUSE by using the standard packaging system, as well as for other distros such as Alpine or CentOS by downloading it directly.

- You can use the package manager Chocolatey to install Perl 6 in Windows; simply type `choco install rakudostar`. This includes only the Rakudo∗ releases, which are the preferred way to use Perl 6.

- If you have Mac with HomeBrew installed, a similar command will get Perl 6 up and running: `brew install rakudostar`.

These and other third-party distributions are listed at `https://perl6.org/downloads/others.html`. See Table 1-1 for more information.

Table 1-1. *Download Information*

Operating system	Instructions
All	Download from `https://rakudo.org/files`
Linux	Instructions at `https://github.com/nxadm/rakudo.pkg`
Windows	`choco install rakudostar`
Mac	`brew install rakudostar`

Perl 6 Online

Containers and rakudo.js, the (WIP) implementation of Perl 6 in JavaScript, have made it very easy to run Perl 6 online. The following online REPLs (Read, Eval, Print Loop) allow you to test your scripts on the go, or in a foreign machine:

- Glot.io at `https://glot.io/new/perl6`. Just insert a line just like this one and click the Run button. You can also save your snippets and publish them.

  ```
  "Hello".comb.map( * ~ 0x20E3.chr ).join().say
  ```

- tio.run has a Perl 6 engine at `https://tio.run/#perl6`. Insert the code above below the Code label and click the Play icon. The output, H☐e☐1☐1☐o☐, will be shown below Output, with some statistics also shown in Debug.

- Ideone (at `ideone.com`) lists Perl 6 as "Perl" in the Others section. Cut and paste the code above, type Ctrl+Enter or click Submit, and you'll get the output in the `stdout` slot. This one even allows interactive programs to run, offering a standard input slot tagged `stdin`. Change the program above to

  ```
  $*IN.comb.map( * ~ 0x20E3.chr ).join().say
  ```

  and write something as input before clicking Submit, and you'll get your input surrounded by squares, same as the Hello in the previous program.

The most interesting of these, although somewhat experimental for the time being, is 6pad: `https://perl6.github.io/6pad/`. This is an actual copy of Perl 6 running on your browser, and for now (beginning of 2019) it's working, but not complete. Just type or paste your program on the left side panel, which is open to the PERL 6 tab and click Run. As an added bonus, you can get HTML output directly, as is done in one of the last Advent Calendar entries at https://perl6advent.wordpress.com/2018/12/07/ with cellular automata.

By the time you read this book, which sat, all alone, in your pile below "Getting things done" and the seventh tome of *A Song of Ice and Fire*, those URLs might no longer exist. However, there will probably be a more stable implementation of Rakudo.js and/or you will be able to set up a container-based sandboxed environment on your own. At any rate, there will be a way to run your code online and share it for demonstration purposes, which is the main objective of these sites.

The Internet is wider than the Web, and there are other places where you can check your scripts, mainly your one-liners, thanks to a series of bots that are able to evaluate Perl 6 and are listening on several IRC channels.

I will talk about IRC and these channels more extensively in the next chapter. For the time being, you might be interested in the next paragraph only if you're already a frequent IRC user.

I will talk about them later on, but there's a channel called #whateverable in Freenode that is entirely dedicated to running these bots. The Camelia bots evaluate your code using the last compiled version of Perl 6, as shown in Figure 1-1.

```
  jmerelo | m: say "Hello, world".comb.map( * ~ 0x35e.chr).join
evalable6 | jmerelo, rakudo-moar c9fe9463e: OUTPUT: «Hello, world"¦»
```

Figure 1-1. Using Camelia (a.k.a. Evalable) from the Weechat IRC client

Command Line (and Other) Options

It's about time you run your own little program, right? Just type perl6 (if you have installed from source, from a binary package, or some other thing) or something that includes running a Docker container if that's what you have used. Either way, you will find a command line, as shown in Figure 1-2.

```
doc [master] % perl6
To exit type 'exit' or '^D'
> █
```

Figure 1-2. *Perl 6 from the command line*

If you have the command-line editing plugin installed (which is standard with Rakudo∗, but not with other options), you will be able to edit your input using the left and right cursors and access previous commands via the up/down arrows.

From that command line, you can

- Write expressions that will be evaluated directly

- Write statements whose result will be printed on the next line

For instance, just write "Hello." This is a literal expression, and it will be printed as such. Write "Hello" ~ ", " ~ "world", and the expression, which concatenates the three strings together, will be evaluated and the result printed. This is the Perl 6 REPL and it will read, evaluate (as an expression or as a statement), and print the result.

Although it's fully functional, you will probably need to run Perl 6 scripts from other scripts, or just repeatedly run them. You can do so from the command line with perl6 -e. So

```
> perl6 -e "'hello'.comb.put"
```

runs that little script that *combs* or divides the string in its letters and prints the result. Since the result is a list, it appears as simply a group of letters separated by whitespace. Since this is an actual program, you can pass arguments to it:

```
> perl6 -e "@*ARGS.join.comb.put" hello world
h e l l o w o r l d
```

The @*ARGS array contains all arguments that you have passed, in this case hello world, joins them, and then separates by letter, which is the result you see printed.

Perl6 --help returns all the options that are available from the command line. Some are intended for advanced users, but some are quite interesting for any kind of user:

- -v or --version prints the version number. You are going to need this every time you ask a question, since one of the first things people need to know is the version you are working with. It prints

  ```
  This is Rakudo version 2018.12 built on MoarVM
  version 2018.12
  implementing Perl 6.d.
  ```

  This message states the fact that every Perl 6 interpreter is composed of Rakudo (which is the actual program that parses yours) and a virtual machine, in this case MoarVM. Besides saying which versions are being used, it says the *specification* it is following, in this case 6.d. Perl 6 versions changes from time to time, with the first production-ready version called 6.c (Christmas), and the newly released one 6.d (Diwali). 6.e does not yet have a scheduled time for publication.

- -c checks the syntax of a program, printing Syntax OK if it checks out. It's useful if that's the only thing you want, or you want to check foreign code for correctness. Please bear in mind that this does not mean it checks *all* possible errors, just those that can be detected statically by reading the source without actually *running* it. However, this does not mean that the syntax check will not compile anything. Some code is executed at the compile phase, so this

```
perl6 -c -e "BEGIN { say «Gotcha» }"
```

prints Gotcha before Syntax OK. See Table 1-2 for a summary.

Table 1-2. *Functions and Commands*

Function	Command line flag
Run from command line	-e
Help on CLI flags and options	--help
Check syntax only	-c
Print Perl 6 version	-v/--version

Concluding Remarks

For most people, the Rakudo Star distributions are the best option. Please use them either as a REPL or for running (at this stage) your one-liners from the command line.

Since Perl 6 is an interpreted language without a default IDE, running it from the command line in a terminal is the right way of using it, and you will do so in this book.

CHAPTER 2

Getting Help

How to Get Your Questions Answered and Start Becoming a Part of the Big Perl Community

No technical book is complete without an exposition of where and how you can go beyond it to find help when you want to know more, or simply when you hit a bump on your road to learning. And help is right there at your fingertips; however, it's not obvious at first sight which sources are the most authoritative or how to interact with them to get to an answer that is not already available. In this chapter, I will talk about these sources and how to leverage them to know more about Perl 6.

First Responders

These are the first places you should look up to get your questions answered and your problems solved. And first among equals, check out the official documentation for Perl 6, which is online at `https://docs.perl6.org/`. It includes a helpful search slot in the upper right corner where you can look up terms that have already been indexed (such as *string*) or search the whole site for any group of words or sentences; the last option in the drop-down menu is always "search the whole site." If your query has not been indexed, it will say "Not in index, try site search," which will return, via Google, all pages in the domain that include that word. For instance, searching for Ubuntu will return this page: `https://docs.perl6.org/language/5to6-perlvar`.

© J.J. Merelo 2019
J.J. Merelo, *Perl 6 Quick Syntax Reference*, https://doi.org/10.1007/978-1-4842-4956-7_2

The documentation is divided into several sections, with their own front pages. The *Language* section (https://docs.perl6.org/language. html) includes tutorials and pages that introduce you to concepts using examples; the pages listed under the *At the beginning* heading may be particularly helpful. The functions and data types are listed under the *Types* and *Routines* headings; you'll find an exhaustive listing of all, well, types and routines and what they do. They are better used as a reference, or via the little search facility. When someone tells you to RTFM, they probably mean this part. While, in general, the Perl 6 community tries to avoid that kind of behavior, it is not a bad idea to at least know where to find things like the official reference.

Since this is a big thing, including nearly 100K lines, it's not installed by default when you download Perl 6 (as seen in the previous chapter), but you can always get your own local version using

```
zef install p6doc
```

The documentation and its website are also available as a Docker container. If you type

```
docker run --rm -it -p 3000:3000 jjmerelo/perl6-doc
```

on the command line, it will start running the content of https://docs. perl.org in port 3000 of your local host. After running this for the first time, it will store the image locally so you can keep consulting it any time you want.

After the documentation, you can always trust Good Ol' Google to answer your questions about Perl 6. Make sure you type "Perl 6" or "perl6" with quotes to get the answer about your questions in the correct language. For instance, "How to save to a file in perl 6" will return the Perl 6 documentation page on input/output https://docs.perl6.org/ language/io.

You can also use the programmer-and-privacy friendly DuckDuckGo. However, again, type "Perl 6" with quotes. DuckDuckGo highlights search results found in Stack Overflow, and in this case it returns this page on how to read and write XLSX files: `https://stackoverflow.com/questions/48050617/what-perl-6-modules-can-read-write-xlsx-files#48051038`. This answer is less than awesome, but your mileage may vary with other queries.

Trying the same query with another search engine, Bing, will return all kinds of results, mostly unrelated to Perl 6. Yandex, the search engine of Russian origin, does return several pages that deal with Perl 6 but none related to how to save a file. At the end of the day, if you are going to use a search engine to seek answers to problems in Perl 6, it's better if you stick to Google.

On the other hand, there are other ways to get answers for questions that have not been answered before. Stack Overflow, which is shown as a sidebar in DuckDuckGo, is the go-to site for every kind of programmer. It has a "karma" mechanism that rewards users who offer good questions and answers. The Perl 6 community is very active on Stack Overflow, using mainly perl6 and related tags, such as Rakudo, MoarVM, or NativeCall.

In general, it is also very friendly and helpful, answering with links to documentation or tutorials and well-motivated articles. It always helps, however, if you follow a few rules when formulating your question:

- State clearly your intention. Your question might imply a way to solve your original problem that may not be the best. Stating your goal will help the responder give you some other possible venues to get there.

- *Golf* your problem to the minimal program that can reproduce it. It is difficult for anybody wanting to help to wade through 20 lines of code, out of which just three or four are needed to reproduce it. Cutting and pasting your code should be enough to run it and reproduce the result, too.

- Paste the output you obtained literally and in text form, so that other people searching for the same error will be able to get to your question and be helped by the answers.

- Show everything you have tested. If there are similar questions answered in Stack Overflow (which will show up as you write it) link to them and explain why your question is different from them.

- If there is an answer that pretty much covers your question, accept it by clicking the tick mark. This will help other people to find the answer to their problem, if it is like yours. Also, be generous by voting up comments and other answers if they are helpful.

Sometimes you need the answer now, and it is neither in the Internet somewhere nor in Stack Overflow; you might have asked the question there but you didn't get any answer in a short period of time. You might want to try something else.

IRC Channels and Other Online Communities

In Chapter 1, I made a reference to IRCs as a place where you could get snippets of Perl 6 code run. You might have skipped that part if you didn't know what IRC was. Here and now you really need to know how to use it, but before you get to your nearest internet-connected device to look up IRC, let's get to other resources you are probably using already, like email. The perl6-users mailing list, `https://lists.perl.org/list/perl6-users.html`, includes most developers and lots of users, and is also a good place to ask your questions and get them answered. Before posting any question, it helps to search the archives at `www.nntp.perl.org/group/perl.perl6.users/`. It always helps to do your homework first via the aforementioned first responders and the documentation. Although nobody in this community will answer with a RTFM (read the fine manual), showing that you have actually read the manual and it does not solve your needs will help the person answering to get it right, and of course the people who write the manuals (who are also listening) can improve them so that next time most questions are actually answered in it.

Then, there is IRC.

I make a little pause here because you might not know about IRC. You know enough about Telegram or Slack. Well, IRC is your grandma's Slack: it stands for Internet Relay Chat, and from a user point of view it includes a set of channels that are denoted by the now-ubiquitous hash, #, and are hosted on a series of servers, of which the most famous in the free software community is probably FreeNode (`https://freenode.net`). Thus, the coordinates of an IRC channel include a node (like above) and a hash-name, like #perl6. This is precisely *the* go-to place for people who want to get help and generally discuss or simply hang out with Perl 6 aficionados.

If you have not heard about IRCs before, you will probably need some help getting there too. The easiest way is to use `https://perl6.org/IRC`, a web-based client. Apart from proving that you are not a robot, evil or otherwise, you just need a browser to access the channel. Sometimes you might feel as if you are barging into the middle of a conversation (which is, as a matter of fact, the case), so checking the logs at `https://colabti.org/irclogger/irclogger_logs/perl6` will give you some background of what happened before you came in.

If you eventually get to use it with a certain frequency, you might want to get your very own IRC client. I favor WeeChat, which can be configured to your usual (and authenticated) username and password, but you might want to use any of those recommended here: `https://opensource.com/life/15/11/top-open-source-irc-clients`. As you get further into the community, it is a good habit to hang out in the IRC channel to help others, as well as get help. Besides, IRC, as any other chat application,

includes helpful *bots* that automatically respond to some questions.
The perl6 IRC channel is no exception, hosting a whole bot herd, of which
Camelia is the most useful (I mentioned her in Chapter 1). Camelia
evaluates Perl 6 expressions and answers with the output. You can invoke
Camelia by writing m: at the beginning of a line, like this:

```
+xIIII | more like parse times, but that's the lion's share o
+jmerelo | m: say "Are you Camelia?"
+camelia | rakudo-moar d39e2fc4f: OUTPUT: «Are you Camelia?␤»
```

In the next line, Camelia will answer with a message that states the
combination of Perl she is using, along with the commit hash that has been
used to compile it (that is, the actual version of the compiler used), and
then the answer preceded by OUTPUT.

That answer gets in the middle of a conversation, and it's generally
not considered good etiquette to start a long conversation with her. So,
there is another channel, #whateverable, which is specifically devoted
to that kind of thing, chatting with bots. Use your online client to /join
#whateverable or do it from the web client, whatever suits you the best.

The following blog will keep you updated, week by week, of happenings
in the Perl 6 community: "Weekly changes in and around Perl 6" by
Liz Mattijsen at https://p6weekly.wordpress.com/. It mentions all
developments in the Perl 6 core and surroundings, current events, and
comments from all over the Web and social media. If you have an account
in WordPress, you can subscribe to it, or just check it whenever you feel like.
Also, near Christmas, the Perl 6 Advent Calendar publishes tutorials and
small articles on Perl 6 lore, sometimes with a tongue-in-cheek title and
attitude. They go all the way back to 2009, so there are lots of articles to learn
from, comment on, or like; go to https://perl6advent.wordpress.com/.

There is a sizable community on Facebook at www.facebook.com/
groups/perl6/, who, while mainly devoted to community and article
announcements, will be happy to answer your questions too. People go

there for first-time orientation, and Wendy van Dijk and the rest of the admins and users will happily help you get your questions answered. This is probably the best place to get a feel of Perl 6 as a community, not simply as a programming language.

Most Perl 6 developers have an account on Twitter, and you can ask for help there. Just using #perl6 as a hashtag will probably draw the attention of one or another, but the go-to account is @perl6org. I will be also happy to help at @jjmerelo.

Last, but by no means least, is the /r/perl6 subreddit at www.reddit.com/r/perl6/, which is also a clearinghouse for articles published elsewhere, and sometimes heated discussions on technical (and not) issues. This is the only original part of the site, since it's a place where you post links to elsewhere. Of all the resources, this is one you might want to skip, since discussions here can get too heated at times. But if you are already a Reddit user, subscribing and contributing to it will help you get fresh news about everything happening everywhere else in Perl 6 land.

You might also learn from looking at examples and get feedback if you submit your own; one of the most active places is Exercism.io at https://exercism.io/tracks/perl6; the Perl 6 track includes all kinds of mentor and community-proposed exercises, along with a simple way to check if they are correct or not. Since Perl 6 is a very expressive language, you will find that Perl solutions figure a lot of times in the rankings of Code-Golf.io. However, unless authors choose to publish them, they are not visible on the site. For instance, one author chose to publish his here: https://gist.github.com/mcreenan/ed62d5e743e18d9e91bb87ba3675dc6e.

Just searching for "perl 6 examples" will give you lots of repositories to choose from, but my advice is to first think about particular tasks or problems you want to solve, and then do a search or use all these resources to walk through getting closer to the solution.

Getting Help in the Physical World

Local Perl user groups have been called Perl Mongers from the beginning of time. They are not ubiquitous, but there are several active ones in major cities and in the capital cities of many countries. Active Perl Mongers hold monthly technical, and sometimes social, meetings. Maybe the best known is in London, but some other active Perl Mongers include Los Angeles, Amsterdam, Cincinnati, Portland, Toronto, and Austin; some of them have been active for more than 20 years. Also, most of them are focused on our sister language, Perl 5 (or simply Perl), and might not have tried Perl 6. Community-wise, however, they are friendly places where you can discuss development in general or present your latest project, pet or not.

In that sense, some other user groups are open to all kinds of people interested in development, but your mileage might vary. Google Developer Groups, for instance, have a focus on Google products, although all kinds of developers are (usually) welcome. This is why you might want to take a trip to attend conferences focused on Perl, of which there is probably one somewhere in the world every month. Major ones, however, are The Perl Conference, which takes place yearly in June in the United States, YAPC (Yet Another Perl Conference)::Japan, which takes place by the end of January, and what is now going to be called PerlCon and is held in early August somewhere in Europe. Since they are devoted to Perl at large, Perl 6 is a small, but growing, part of them, but still most core developers will be there; there are usually tutorials the previous days, and sometimes hackathons take place after the conference, so plan for a whole week. Getting acquainted with projects using Perl 6 in production and learning new features always has some value. And there are always stickers to carry home or, even better, to add to your laptop. It is also the best way to get help face-to-face with the person who wrote or documented the thing you are interested in.

If you are looking further than getting acquainted with the language and want actual hands-on problem solving from a consultant, there are many individuals that can help you, but their quantity and availability might vary, so you might want to use one of the other virtual or physical venues to check them out. At the time of writing, Edument offers Perl 6 consultancy through `Perl6.services`; it is based in Prague, the Czech Republic. Nigel Hamilton also offers practical Perl 6 training from his company, based in the UK: `https://nigelhamilton.com/perl6.html`.

Concluding Remarks

From documentation to consultants to getting your questions answered in a rapid and efficient way, Perl 6 offers all kinds of facilities to newcomers and seasoned programmers alike. Perl 6 is the kind of language you check out due to the technology, but you keep using thanks to the community. Let's delve into that technology in the next chapter.

CHAPTER 3

Literals

How Simple Data Is Typed and How Perl 6 Understands It

Let's start by understanding how expressions are built in Perl 6. Expressions are the building blocks of statements, which in turn are the basic building blocks of programs, and they can be directly interpreted by the REPL. This is a good starting point for understanding the syntax and general intent of the language and how it can be used to solve simple problems. But first,

Let's Talk About Unicode

Perl 6 has been designed to work from Unicode from the ground up. So, you need to know a bit about it before you can understand how expressions are built and used.

Unicode is a consortium that, although better known for its regular admission of new emojis, is actually in charge of how literal information is represented inside computers. In the beginning, Unicode assigned a number for every symbol in every alphabet known to humankind, including not only letters and numbers, but also ligatures and symbols. Some commonly used symbols, like typographic symbols, were thrown in for good measure, and eventually emojis and newly popular symbols were added. So, at a first level, every character has a unique number assigned to it, which guarantees that it is interpreted in the same way by every program and operating system. Thus, 幺 is always the number 12083. Additionally, every character, or *codepoint*, which is its proper denomination, also has a name, which is usually represented in all capital letters. The codepoint above is called `KANGXI RADICAL SHORT THREAD`, for instance.

You can look up character names in your editor if it has the correct plugin. Atom includes the character-table package, for instance; VS-code has a plugin called Insert Unicode, and emacs can access character names by pressing Control-x + 8 + Return + tab and then using control-s to search in a single document. There is also an index in alphabetical order at `http://unicode.org/charts/charindex.html`.

Every codepoint also has a set of *properties*, which are hints of what it is able to do and how to connect it with other codepoints. Think of properties as labels or tags that say, for those who do not actually know the alphabet, what the codepoint is. Is it a number? Is it a symbol? Is it a letter, and, if so, what kind of letter? These kinds of properties might become important when sorting or simply combining codepoints to form complex words or ciphers or whatever the combination of those symbols is actually called. For instance, digits can be put together with other digits to form numbers, which assign a value depending on position. But you can't combine them with *numbers* because they have a single, stand-alone value.

You don't normally see codepoints, but *graphemes*, which can be understood as a rendering of a codepoint, also as a first approximation. But a grapheme can also be a group of codepoints; in some cases, it can be both. For instance, we Spanish-speaking people love our ñ (we call it eh-gne), which is called in Unicode `LATIN SMALL LETTER N WITH TILDE`. The name already implies that it's a letter, n, which includes another Unicode symbol, the tilde. As a matter of fact, there's a whole set of symbols that can't be printed if they are not combined with other symbols; in this case, it's called the combining tilde. So, the alternative way of representing this symbol is to use two codepoints, the n and the combining tilde; note that the single codepoint and the two codepoints use the same grapheme, ñ.

Something similar happens with emojis and with what is called a name sequence.

These descriptions are also included in the Unicode *properties*, which are a set of characteristics a codepoint has. Those properties describe whether is a *small* (lowercase) or *capital* (uppercase) letter, among other properties, so that it's able to identify if a codepoint is using the same letter despite all the additional symbols (like tildes) or cases (upper, lower, and others used in different alphabets).

You don't need to worry about this right now, but Unicode will show up over and over again on this chapter (and in most of the rest of the book), so having this small introduction in mind will help you understand much of what is going on under, and sometimes over, the hood when Perl 6 parses your code. Remember always that *Unicode is important*, and it will be essential in understanding how dealing with any kind of written data, numbers, letters, or any kind of symbols, works in Perl 6.

Literal Expressions

Literal expressions are, *literally*, what they seem to be. If they look like a number, they *are* a number; if they look like a string, they *are* a string. However, Perl 6 is quite rich in the kind of things that can be represented literally. You can use the REPL to just type these literal expressions. If they are correct, they will be printed back to you in the next line; that way you can experiment with any kind of expressions.

Numbers and Digits

Let's start with numbers. Besides *usual* numbers like 3, 4.5, or .35, *fractions* can also be represented literally. ¾ is a valid literal, rational number, as is 3/4 and they are worth the same (and are the same as 0.75).

Characters like ¾ are called *composites*, and there are different ways to enter them from your keyboard. They generally involve selecting one key (for instance, the Right-Control key) as a prefix to indicate the next two keys are going to be composed; in some cases, an additional application might be needed. Please consult your OS and windowing environment online help to find out how to do this. In many cases, your editor will be able to do this (although only while you're working in it) and there's always the fallback option to display a set of Unicode characters from your operating system or online.

Numbers can also be represented as superscripts, but when they are, they also act as an *operation*. The ^{2} in 3^2 means "squared." If it's used by itself, it simply means 2.

By default, and if possible, floating point numbers are represented as rationals, since Perl 6 considers this is a more precise way of representing them. However, you can explicitly ask for a floating point representation by using the "e" form, as in 1e0; this means $1*10^0$, and exp(0) is precisely 1. 1E6 is 1 million and is represented also as a floating-point number. In general, the literal you use to write a number affects its representation, but not its value. 1E6, 1000000, and 1000000/1 have the same numeric value, although they are internally represented in different ways, using different types.

These are, effectively, different *types* in Perl 6. This is a concept that we will be getting into in depth in the next chapters.

Complex numbers are another type that can be represented literally; they have two components, the "real" and the "imaginary" part. 3+.5i is such a number, and you can use it as such in Perl 6.

All languages also need to use, from time to time, usually when they are dealing with the content of messages from other machines, numbers in hexadecimal, octal, or binary; the first two are often found in the description of colors, and the latter is basic Computerese and thus found in many operations. A 0 followed by the initial is used: 0b precedes binary numbers, 0x hexadecimal numbers, and 0o octal numbers. Thus, 0b1111, 0xF, and 0o17 represent the same number, our well-known 15.

Conventionally, hexadecimal numbers use capital letters; however, the prefix 0xf is as valid as the version shown.

Besides this feat of representing numbers in the most usual bases (also known as radices, plural for radix), something that is shared with almost every other language, Perl 6 is also able to represent any base using the :number prefix and the number between square brackets. With this notation, :3<120> is again 15 and :17<f> the same. For lack of (Latin) characters to represent them, you can't go any further than base 36, where :36<zz> is 1295.

But numbers in Perl 6 are not limited to Western digits. As mentioned, the language has full support of Unicode, and while I am not going to fully explain what this means for the time being, it implies that a number in any script will also behave as numbers. Some numbers you can also try:

- Roman script: ⅭⅭ (which is, indeed, the first time I have seen this symbol) is equivalent to 100,000, for instance, besides the (probably known from clocks and suchlike) I, V, X. However, you can't just juxtapose these figures to form numbers the way you do in clocks: while XI is correct (but a single codepoint), XI is not.

- Circled numbers also behave as their uncircled equivalent: ⑱ behaves just the same way as 18. There are all kinds of numbers and digits, with many kinds of highlights, such as the so-called "mathematical bold digits," like this one: **5**. However, juxtaposition will not work, same as above.

- Arabic numbers can also be used: ٢ for two, for instance. In this case, juxtaposition will work: ٢٥ is equal to 25. Some other scripts, like the Khmer script, have the same quality: ៥៨ is 58. In general, you will be able to form numbers using codepoints that have the "digit" quality; not all numbers do. The ones mentioned above, for instance, don't, which is why juxtaposition will not work for forming numbers. Roman script is not actually a positional system, which explains why it does not work either. There are, all in all, 33 alphabets that include digits, and they include the Tibetan, Myanmar, and Bengali alphabets, plus others that are not so well known.

In all these cases, it is not enough to use a "compose" key to type those graphemes. You need an editor that allows searching by name and then writing these digits. Most developer editors include this facility either in their basic configuration or as a plug-in. And although you might think your usual digits are more than enough for all your computing needs, you never know when you will land a job where you will need to write numbers in the vernacular. Since there are many different versions of the Latin alphabet (actually of Arabic origin) digits, you may want to use them for decoration or emphasis.

Two special numbers, or rather two special not-numbers, are available in Perl 6: NaN, which means "Not a Number," and Infinity, which is represented either by Inf or by the actual symbol, ∞. NaN is different from any other number, and ∞ is bigger than any other number. Having an explicit, and literal, representation for them allows you to use them as default values in expressions, and also as a return of expressions that will be mathematically correct.

In the same vein, and certainly not a number, but also not everything else, is *Nil*, which is how undefined values should be called in this language. You can use it to nullify the value of a variable, or to indicate there's no value.

It's not exactly a literal, but a class, which can also be typed directly. There's a reason for it being so, but it's mentioned in this section since it's functionally similar to the literals described above.

Enumerated Values

In some cases, sets of objects that can take a finite and well-defined number of values are grouped in what is called an enumerated value. There are a few of them in Perl 6, but I will describe just two in this section. You can write them as such in Perl 6, and the interpreter will understand them.

Logic or Boolean are one of these types and take just two values: a Boolean value is either true or false, so it can be simply represented by True or False. Capitalization is important.

The result of a comparison can take three different values: for two things, either they are the same, the first is bigger than the other, or the other way round. These values are used in a Perl 6 enumerated type called Order, and they are represented by the literals Less, Same, and More.

Other types, such as the state of a file or the status of a promise also use enumerated values, but they need concepts that will be explained later in the book.

Strings

String literals are usually enclosed in quotes. However, and in the spirit of
Unicode support, quoting can be done in many ways. "Hey" is as valid as
«Hey» and as good as your good old "Hey" or 'Hey'. Other styles of quotes,
such as the German (and Japanese) 「a」 or the paired typographic quotes
"a" can also be used. I will use " for simplicity, but any set of single, double,
or paired quotes can be used to define string literals in Perl 6. There is a
difference, however, between simple or double quotes, and it is related to
how they deal with interpolation and escape characters (which you will see
later).

Also, in the spirit of Unicode support, you can use any codepoint in
string literals, like "12three", "二重鉤括弧", or even combine different
scripts, like "二重鉤括弧사과·". Actual quotes need to be *escaped* with a
backslash "This is a quote \"". The so-called *escape characters* can also be
used. See Table 3-1.

Table 3-1. *Escape Characters*

Escape character	Meaning
\a	Bell. Makes a system-defined sound.
\b	Backspace. Moves back the space of a single character.
\t	Tab. Moves forward the space of a tab stop (system-dependent, but generally four spaces).
\n	Newline. Moves to the next line.
\f	Form feed. Equivalent to moving to the next page, but the actual meaning depends on the context.
\r	Carriage return. Moves to the beginning of the line.
\e	Used for escape codes, which are used, for instance, for inserting color.

An additional escape character, \x, followed by a number, is used to directly access Unicode characters: "\x062b" prints ث and "\x231b" prints ⌛.

Additionally, escape sequences starting with \c followed by square brackets can also be used to create literal sequences of codepoints by their official name or numeric representation, which is a number literal. For instance, "\c[0x1F600]" prints 😀. You could also type "\c[128512]", which is the decimal equivalent. As a matter of fact, you can even use this for concatenating several codepoints: "\c[128512,128514,128516,128518]" prints 😀😂😄😆. This capability is very similar to that of \x, but \c goes further by allowing also for an official description of the codepoint or combination of codepoints, like "\c[TAMIL SYLLABLE VAA]", which is equivalent to வா.

All these forms can be combined in a single string literal: "\c[0x1F600] Hi\x062b" has three codepoints and prints as 😀Hiث.

Note   Unicode codepoint names are defined by the Unicode consortium, but in many cases, you can look them up in your editor.

There are differences with respect to how simple and double quotes deal with the escape sequences above. While double quotes behave as indicated, simple quotes just let them through, with '\x062b' representing exactly that sequence of characters, and \c-escaped characters dealt with in the same way. Still, both interpret escape characters, which are mainly characters that have some syntactical meaning, such as the quotes themselves. 'Hi \' escaped character' works the same in simple and double quotes. If you want to have a literal sequence, the Q[] quoting construct does exactly that. Differences in behavior are shown in Table 3-2.

Table 3-2. *Escape Character Details*

Quote	Escape character	Escape sequence
Single quote, '	Processed	As-is
Double quote, "	Processed	Processed
Literal quote, Q[]	As-is	As-is

Pairs

These literals are not "atomic" as above, since they are literally composed of several literals. However, since they *literally* create a single object, which is called a pair in Perl 6, we consider them literal in the same way we consider complex numbers literals.

Key-value pairs are also literals in Perl 6. They are use throughout many functions, so there's a convenient way to express them using the *fat arrow* symbol. The key must be a string, and the value can be anything. Since so far you have seen only string and numeric literals, let's use them.

```
"Today" => "6 pounds"
"Tomorrow" => 3/5
```

Additionally, if the key is only composed of letters, dashes (-), apostrophes ('), underscores (_), and numbers not preceded by a dash, the quotes used in the key can be eliminated:

```
Today-ain't-day_1 => "No it ain't"
```

There's a special kind of pair called a *colon pair* because it starts with a colon. :so represents a pair with key of so and a value of True. The colon must be followed by a string that matches the same description as above; so :Today-ain't-day1 is equivalent to Today-ain't-day1 => True. This pair is also called an *adverbial pair* since it has the same form as adverbs.

How can you express the opposite, a `False` value? Since `!` is equivalent to negation in most languages (including Perl 6), putting it between the colon and the key will negate its value: `:!Today-ain't-day1` makes it `False` instead of `True`.

This kind of literal is not limited to logical values. Using a number is also an abbreviated way to express a pair whose value is numeric: `:42street`, for instance. This is equivalent to a pair where the key is street and the value is 42. Perl 6 parses this by finding where the number ends and the letters start, so it's equivalent to `street => 42`; it can also be written as `:street(42)`.

```
:42street === ("street" => 42)        # True
:street(42) === :42street             # True
```

Is It a String? Is It a Number? It's an *Allomorph!*

According to the Wikipedia, an allomorph is a variant form of a morpheme. However, in Perl 6, it is something that can work either as a number or as a string, depending on how you use it. In practice, they are numbers surrounded by the special <> quotes. <42> is such an allomorph, while <33.5> or <55e55> are other valid ways of writing them. In general, any valid literal number surrounded by <> is a valid allomorph. You can pad the number with any number of spaces and it retains the same result.

Versions

Versions are important artefacts in Perl 6, since they are used as metadata for classes; often it's useful to known whether an installed version is older than the version you want to install, for instance. That is why (among other reasons) they get their own literals, which start with the letter v in lowercase, followed by a digit or group of digits (in any script), optionally followed by numbers or letters separated by dots. It might include asterisks between two dots, but nowhere else, and a plus sign as a suffix to indicate it might be that version or newer ones. All of the following are valid version strings:

```
v0.0.1
v0.0.2.rc2.v3.this.is.the.good.one
v2019.*
v2018.1+
v3.π
v៥      # KHMER DIGIT FIVE
```

These, however, aren't valid:

```
vπ.3
v8.3    # Includes an Unicode 8. character
vVII    # Roman numerals are not digits.
```

Concluding Remarks

Understanding how a language groks data is essential to build upon data handling and eventually processing. In this chapter, you learned how to type numeric and string data, and how Unicode plays a part in that.

You will learn how to operate with data in the next chapter.

CHAPTER 4

Expressions and Operators

Understanding Simple Expressions and How They Are Built

Once you know how to enter basic data into Perl 6, the next natural step is to build expressions with them. This is what you will learn in this chapter, where, as in the previous one, code and expressions can be typed in the REPL and the result will be printed on the next line if there's no error, as shown in Figure 4-1.

```
Perl6QR % perl6
To exit type 'exit' or '^D'
> -38_000_000
-38000000
> █
```

Figure 4-1. *Typing an expression into the REPL, which returns the evaluated value*

Basic Expressions

Basic expressions are combinations of operators and literals. Most languages use operators in the middle of their operands, like 3+2. They are called *infix* operators. In many cases, *prefix* operators like -2 are used too.

Perl 6 adds a host of new kinds of operators:

- *Postfix* operators are *behind* their operand.

- *Circumfix* operators are placed *before and behind* their operand, parenthesis style.

- *Postcircumfix* operators are *behind* (that's the post part) and around (the *circum* part) their operands.

The most common operators you are going to explore in this chapter are in-, pre-, and postfix.

Since Perl 6 makes full use of Unicode, in many cases you will be able to use operators in the same way you would in Math or Physics; they go on top of the regular, plain vanilla operators we use every day. That is why it's convenient, if you haven't yet, to configure your system for typing general Unicode characters, composed or not.

For this section of the chapter, let's use the Perl 6 command line (local or online) as a simple calculator. Type the expressions (in the example or any variation you might think of), press Enter, and the REPL will do its 'E' thing and print the result.

Arithmetic

These expressions involve numbers. Although any number can be used, for the sake of coherence with the language this book is written in, I'll use regular numbers composed of decimal digits.

Let's start with the simplest *prefix* operator: the – sign converts a positive number into a negative one, like so:

-⅗

-7

-33.5

-38_000_000

All of these numbers are valid negative rational, integer, floating-point, or big numbers. Underscores are used simply for visual grouping.

Let's revisit the concept of allomorphs, which I defined in the last chapter. In these circumstances, they behave as a number, so -< 42 > is the same as 42.

Arithmetic operators, in general, go in the middle of their operands: they are *infix* operators. They will work if whatever is in there is a number:

3+7

2-⅔

⅓*⅔

3.234/3

All of these numbers produce a value that belongs to the type of the most complex of the two, which, in most cases, is a rational number.

The fact that Perl 6 uses rationals by default means that, unlike many other languages, expressions like 0.3+0.6-0.9 are precisely 0, while Python returns -1.1102230246251565e-16.

Rationals are used by default for most numbers, unless the numerator or denominator is excessively big.

By big I mean a numerator or denominator less than 1 followed by 19 zeros. You probably don't need to worry about that.

Perl 6 is also unusual in the way it uses exponentiation. x ** y is the usual x raised to the y-th power, but you can also use the power of Unicode (no pun intended) to write 3^{22}, meaning 3 elevated to the 22th power (which is 31381059609).

Perl 6 does have a variety of other operators you can use, which are specific or use a specific notation. They are shown in Table 4-1.

Table 4-1. Other Operators

Operator	What it does
div	Rounding down integer division. 3 div 2 results in 1, but 3 div -2 yields -2.
%	Modulo or remainder operator; the remainder of the integer division. The result of x/y is equal to x div y plus (x % y)/y. Works with any kind of number.
%%	Divisible by. Returns True if a % b is zero.
mod	Integer modulo or remainder operation. Same as %, but both elements must be integers.
gcd	Greatest common divisor. 33 gcd 121 returns 11. Converts their operands into integers. 100/3 gcd 121.9 returns exactly the same, by rounding down 100/3 to 33 and 121.9 to 121.
lcm	Least common multiple. Behaves by rounding down to the nearest integer too. 2018 lcm 2019 returns 4074342, for instance.

Comparison operators probably deserve their own set of paragraphs. Let's go first with equality and inequality. Numeric equality uses ==; operands are compared for *value*, not for literal representation, so 3.0 == 9/3 is effectively True.

Perl 6, as with many other languages, uses == to differentiate it from the assignment operator, =. Mistakenly using the assignment operator as an equality operator yields an error if both sides are literals. It won't in other cases, so better be careful about it.

There's another original operator that checks approximate equality. ≅ or its equivalent, =~=, returns True if the two operands are equal to a tolerance of 1e-15; this is the default value and it can be changed if needed to a smaller (or bigger) value. Thus,

```
1 =~= 1-1/1e16
```

returns True, since 1 is approximately equal to 0.9999999999999999.

Numeric inequality takes three different forms, all of them exactly equivalent: ≠ and their ASCII equivalents, != and !==.

They return if a number is bigger or smaller than another in Boolean fashion. Perl 6 uses less than (<) and bigger than (>) but also *less than or equal* ≤ as well as greater than or equal (≥).

This is the first case in which you are using operators that are written using Unicode codepoints. Perl 6 acknowledges that not everyone will have their keyboard or operating system configured for entering them; this is why every Unicode term or operator has its *ASCII* equivalent.

ASCII is the American Standard Code for the Interchange of Information, which is a Unicode predecessor that included only the Latin alphabet and some usual symbols. They are the symbols that can be easily typed from a keyboard; in this book and the Perl 6 documentation, ASCII basically means using "plain and simple" letters and other characters. That might be the reason why they were called the *Texas* version, but maybe also because "everything is bigger in Texas" and they need several characters as opposed to

Unicode's single codepoint, so they look bigger than the equivalent. Anyhow, in September 2017 all references to Texas were changed to ASCII. You might still find it in older articles, such as this one: `www.learningperl6.com/2016/11/22/quick-tip-7-texas-and-unicode-things/`.

In this case, $\geq$ is equivalent to >= and $\leq$ to <=.

Equivalently, != or $\neq$ means not equal. It is True if the operands are one (whichever) greater than the other.

There is another operator that can be used for ordering numbers, since it returns an order: <=> returns Less, Same, or More depending on the numeric values of its operands. 3 <=> 4 is Less, while 3.0 <=> 9/3 returns Same.

Perl 6 has a couple of original operators: min and max return the smallest and the largest of the arguments, respectively.

All of these arithmetic operators will work on your generic idea of numbers (or numeric types, as they will be called later on in this book). Any attempt to use them on non-numbers might fail. There are two caveats to this, however.

The first one is that enumerated types are, underneath, just numbers.

```
42 + True
```

yields 43, since that is the value it has.

```
33 + Same
```

is still 33, since Same's value is 0; Less is worth -1 and More +1; True is worth also 0.

The second caveat is all of the allomorphs mentioned above are actually numbers in string scaffolding:

```
333 + < 222 >
```

is 555, since the allomorph, in a numeric context, behaves as a number.

As a matter of fact, arithmetic operators put data in a *context* in which conversion to a numeric value is attempted. This is an example of contexts, of which you will see (much) more later. This conversion, or *coercion*, transforms data from a type to another. For instance,

40 + "2"

yields 42, with these things happening under the hood:

- + acts as a *contextualizer*, meaning "this thing here is going to be understood as if it were a number."

- +"2" puts a string (that actually contains a number) in a numeric context, which *coerces* the string to a number, making it behave exactly the same as +2.

In general, all arithmetic operators act as contextualizers in the right conditions. This makes Perl 6 very flexible when acting on data whose literal representation might be something different.

Strings

There are many things you can do with strings in Perl 6. The simplest one is to stick them together, via the ~ operator, so

"Let's go" ~ " to the mall"

creates a new string from those two, with no space in the middle. This works also if any of them, or both, are a number, so

33 ~ "p"

is "33p". This is another example of *coercion*. ~ acts here as a *string contextualizer*, making everything it's related to a string; ~ 3 is actually the string "3".

If what you want is to repeat the same string, use x. So

```
"Let's go now" x 3
```

creates a very insistent petition.

There are also equality and inequality operators. They return True or False. See Table 4-2.

Table 4-2. *Operators*

Operator	Meaning
Lt	Less than
Le	Less than or equal
Gt	Greater than
Ge	Greater than or equal

They are strictly string operators. However, they work on other kind of literals, such as numbers. They won't work as (maybe) expected here: they get converted to strings and then compared. These comparisons will both be True:

```
3 le 4
330 le 4
```

You can also compare strings with specific operators. There are, in fact, three operators that are used to compare strings: leg, coll, and unicmp. You may have to go back to the section on Unicode to understand what's coming. Don't worry. I'll wait for you here.

Unlike the other two, leg (which stands for *less, equal, or greater)* uses lexicographical order. It looks at the Unicode (a number) of the first two letters of the string, and returns More, Less, or Same depending on how they compare. "\x12345" leg "\x12346" always returns Less. This is called *lexicographic* ordering because it uses precisely the order in which the characters are put in the code they are represented with.

For most purposes, these two operators behave in exactly the same way. As a matter of fact, by default they work in the same way, with "a" coll "Z" and "a" unicmp "Z" returning, by default, the same value. However, the main difference is that you can change the behavior of unicmp using runtime configuration options. I'll get back to that later.

Any of these three operators takes the length of the string into account; strings with less characters are always considered less than others with more characters, if they share all characters but the last ones. "a" leg "aa", "a" coll "aa", and "a" unicmp "aa" are always Less, independent of the second letter (or letters) in the string on the right-hand side.

All of the operators in this section *see* allomorphs as numbers. <3> leg <3.0> returns Less because it's smaller lexicographically, same as <40> leg <5>. The other two operators only look at the order in which their digits, seen as letters, are found. And they fail anyway if they are used with a number.

In many cases, however, you will need to compare two things without knowing in advance what kind they belong to. You will see how to deal with that in the next section.

Handling Syntax Errors

If you have been typing some of the expressions proposed above in your REPL (and you might have), it's likely that you have made some typing errors. If that has not been the case, you are a careful person, but it will happen to you sooner or later, either by mistyping or simply because you are trying to write something you though could work, but the language does not understand it that way. For instance, you might have been trying to do something like what is shown in Figure 4-2.

```
> 3 + "p"
Cannot convert string to number: base-10 number must begin with valid digits or
'.' in '⏏p' (indicated by ⏏)
  in block <unit> at <unknown file> line 1
  ▁
```

Figure 4-2. *Attempting to add two things that can't be added*

This is a *syntax* error, as in there's something wrong in the way the statement has been put together. The error arises from the fact that, as indicated above, the + puts the "p" in numeric context, and then the interpreter tries to add the contents of the string to the number. It fails to do so, and it gives you several interesting pieces of information:

- It tells you what it's trying to do: "... convert string to number." That's quite helpful because you know why it failed.

- It also gives you some hints of why that failed. It's trying to *coerce* the string into a number, but it can't because it does not start with a digit or a period (for floating point numbers).

- Additionally, it tells you precisely where it failed: the ⏏ and the character in red tell you exactly where it didn't work out. It was at that point in the string where it looked for either a digit or a period, and decided, well, can't be done.

- Finally, it tells you where it failed in the context of the whole block it's evaluating. In this case, there's a single line, so knowing it happened in line 1 is not so enlightening, but it helps with bigger files like the ones you will see later in this book.

In general, syntax errors and other kinds of interpreter/compiler errors get a bad rep because they kind of indicate you, the user, failed in some way. That bad rep arises from cryptic error messages, and from the fact that they are literally called "errors" or "failures." In most cases, they are misunderstandings, as in the compiler or interpreter failing to understand what you really mean, and that's the approach of Perl 6's misunderstanding messages. They're like "I tried to do what you mean, and I tried this and that way. However, I failed precisely in this point, for this reason." In some cases, they will even suggest you try something else.

This is one of the strong points of Perl 6. Reading carefully and understanding the error messages will take you a long way.

Smart Comparison Operators

Some operators don't require both operands to be of the same kind and will try to check if one is greater than the other for some definition of "great". The cmp operator is a comparison operator that deals with any kind of operand.

```
33 cmp 55       # Less
"330" cmp "55" # Less
"a" cmp 55      # More, number is converted to string
"a" cmp <55>    # Same result, allomorph → string
33 cmp <55>     # Less, the allomorph → number
```

It can even compare pairs:

```
(a => 33) cmp (b => 33)      # Less
(a => 44) cmp (a => 33)      # More
```

It compares the keys, and if they are the same, it compares values, as above.

Note that I have put the pairs in parentheses. This is due to *operator precedence*, that is, the grouping of operators and operands the interpreter will choose based only on position. Operands *stick* to operators with higher precedence, performing that operation before continuing to others with lower precedence; in this case, cmp has higher precedence than the fat arrow used in pairs, which is why I use the parenthesis: to prevent keys from sticking to the operator instead of the arrow.

Two functionally equivalent operators deal with inequalities: before and after; they convert, or coerce, to a common format, and return True or False.

```
"a" before "b"          # True, string comparison
3 before "33"           # True, coerced to number
v3.2 before v2+         # False, version comparison
⅔ after 0.6             # True, 0.66666... > 0.6
```

In general, you use comparison operators when you want to sort a series of objects. Inequality operators are reserved for simple expressions, such as when you want to make a decision.

Comments: The Importance of Documentation

You might have noticed in the section above I use # to *comment* on the output of that particular expression and do so inline. This is, effectively, the format used in Perl 6 for one-line comments, comments that extend to the end of the line.

```
# This is a comment. It ends right here.
```

Comments are a very important part of code. They are used to explain the intent of the accompanying code. And they are so important that in Perl 6, unlike other languages, they are code themselves. Perl 6 looks into the comments and checks what is there, making it available to the interpreter or the reader of the code.

This will become more important later on, as you proceed with the language. For the time being, you don't need to cut and paste that part of the expressions into your interpreter; they will be, to the effect of the output, ignored.

Logic

Logic expressions return True or False. They appear in most programs when some decision must be made. When some function asks for a Boolean or logic value, it is going to be coerced into one, but you can do so explicitly using the operator so:

```
so True     # True
so 33       # True, since it's non-0
so 0        # False; null values are false
so 0.0      # False; ditto
so "True"   # True as any non-empty string
so ""       # False, empty string
so Nil      # False
so <0>      # False
```

In general, zero or null values return False; non-zero, non-empty values return True. In this case, as you can see, allomorphs are interpreted numerically.

The operator not is the exact opposite of so. not so True is, as should be expected, false.

The single-character operators ? and ! behave in the same way:

```
? 1    # True
!True  # False
```

Note that whitespace between the operator and operand is optional and ignored. You can use them and the wordier form indiscriminately, although in general, for experienced programmers, the last method is preferable; this is similar in other languages.

The next logical operator is and, which is true only if both operands are true; after this one, the result of or is True if just one of its operands is. Operands are coerced to Boolean (using so) before evaluating the expression. They can also use &&, || which, for the time being, behaves in the same way.

Concluding Remarks

Operators, together with literals, allow you to use the interpreter as a glorified calculator. If you use the default distribution, it allows you to run over former operations using the up arrow, and easily edit and redo previous operations.

However, the main point of this chapter is to explain how statements are built. Most of them are built from simple expressions, and you must understand how they work, what kind of preparation they perform on operands, and the output, before proceeding to use them in complex, structured data and chained statements.

You will work with structured data next.

CHAPTER 5

Building Up Data

How Complex Data Is Built from Simple Data, and How to Work with It

So far you have been dealing with *simple* data. In general, you will need to work with data that has some internal structure. You will deal with that in this chapter.

In this chapter, you will keep working with the command line; examples are intended to be typed into the REPL, either locally or in some other shape (as seen in Chapter 1).

In this chapter, you will explore two concepts that will be fleshed out later: class (or type) and role. A class describes how objects (or instances) of that class behave and which attributes they contain; We will use the term class and type indistinctly here, since for the time being we are not referring to any object-oriented concept. An object in Perl 6 belongs to a class, or is of a certain type.

Besides, types can *do* a *role* or they can *implement* a role. You can think of roles as partial types, but in fact it means that they will be able to do certain things, independently of the type they actually are. An object will have a single class or type, but it can implement many different roles. Later chapters will be devoted to this; let this be simply an advance that allows you to understand better how certain objects in Perl 6 behave.

© J.J. Merelo 2019
J.J. Merelo, *Perl 6 Quick Syntax Reference*, https://doi.org/10.1007/978-1-4842-4956-7_5

Code Objects

Functional languages are those that make functions and anything that's *callable*, or that can be called, first-class citizens, that is, treated in the same way any other data structure would; in general, functions are first-class citizens if they can be used in place of any other data structure, without needing a special syntax. In order to do that, you need to actually put them physically first in any text that's devoted to them. That is why they are right here, up front in this chapter.

Taken to the minimal expression, a function is something that can be called or *invoked*. They are called Callables in Perl 6; a Callable is a piece of code that takes arguments and produces some result, either returning a value or some other secondary effect, like printing something.

In general, code objects use curly braces around them:

```
{ 'LOL' }
```

This is the simplest kind of code object (Callable) available and is called a block. Blocks include all kinds of code and return the result of evaluating the last expression within it. As with any kind of code, this block can be applied to an argument using parentheses:

```
{ 'LOL' }(3)  # Returns LOL
```

This is evidently useful just as a way of illustrating the syntax for the simplest piece of code possible. Functions usually take some input in the form of arguments and return the result of applying some operation to that input. Blocks get a (single) argument in $_; the value you enter in parentheses will be substituted into $_ inside the block, like so:

```
{ "Hey " ~ $_}("you")  # Hey you
```

I need to say a couple of things about $_, which is the first Perl 6 variable you see in this book; I will devote a full chapter to them later. First, its *shape:* Perl 6 uses *sigils* to indicate what kind of variable you are dealing with. The $ sigil is used for scalar (can you say $calar?) content, which is the content you saw in Chapter 3. The actual *name, or identifier,* of the variable is the single underscore (_) that follows the sigil.

On the other hand, $_ is *the topic* variable, which is to say, in most cases, the default variable. This means that whenever no container for a value is specified, as in the block above, it will go into this default variable. In the case above, the simple block { "Hey " ~ $_ } does not actually define the name of its arguments, so if it gets handed some value, it goes to the topic variable.

It is, however, and as indicated, a scalar and simple variable. What happens if you use two arguments?

```
{ "Hey " ~ $_ }("you", "and me")
```

You get an error: "Too many positionals passed; expected 0 or 1 arguments but got 2."

The defined block is smart enough to know that there are too many arguments. You could work with the default non-scalar variable, but that is going to be left for later, so I will introduce *twigils:*

```
{ "Hey " ~ $^first ~ " and " ~ $^second}("you", "me")
# Hey you and me
```

Twigils are symbols that follow sigils. In this case, the twigil is the caret (^), which is the default for *positional* formal arguments. No matter what you call them, the placeholder variable that goes first in Unicode order will get what goes first, the second what goes second, and so on. You could have called them

```
{ "Hey " ~ $^fourth ~ " and " ~ $^second}("you", "me")
```

and still get the same result, since

```
"fourth" before "second"
```

is True. Arguments are found between parentheses and separated by a comma.

The kind of name you can use for these placeholders is the same you can use as a key for a pair, as seen in Chapter 3; that is, they can start with a letter or an underscore, and be followed by letters, underscores, apostrophes, dashes, and numbers not preceded by a dash. Neither dashes nor apostrophes can be the last character in the name. $^a_1 is valid, while $^a' and $^a-1 are not. Do keep these rules in mind, because you will come back to them later on. I will call strings following this kind of syntax *bare identifiers*, since you are going to use them often in this book.

And speaking about pairs, these positional arguments are not the only kind of arguments you can use. *Named* arguments are actually pairs, with a name (or key) and a value. If you want to use them, the twigil changes to a colon:

```
{"Hey " ~ $:greet ~ ": " ~ $:tell }( greet => 'you', tell =>
'Well...' )
```

Hey you: Well...

Use them if you want to give real names to arguments, or simply if you've got things that are more naturally represented as pairs, such as truth values (which you saw in Chapter 3):

```
{"The answer is " ~ $:greet  }( :!greet )
# The answer is False
```

Being first-class citizens, you are bound to find blocks in many different situations, so there are ways to define them that are even simpler. The block { "Hey " ~ $_ } is equivalent to "Hey " ~ *, although in order to use it, you will need it to be wrapped around parentheses:

```
("Hey " ~ *)("you") # Hey you
```

In Perl 6, the asterisk (*) is actually a class, called Whatever. When used in this context, in an operation or as an argument to a function, it creates an actual object; when used in an operation, it turns the whole block into an instance of a WhateverCode, which is actually a block. This saves the user from creating and naming placeholder variables that actually have no meaning. Besides, you can use as many asterisks as you want:

```
("Hey " ~ * ~ " and " ~ * ~ " and " ~ *)("you", "me", "anyone")
# Hey you and me and anyone
```

The three arguments get transferred to the three instances of Whatever seamlessly. This might get confusing to the untrained eye, as in

```
( * * * ** * )(2,3,4) # 2 * ( 3 ** 4 ) == 162
```

However, Perl 6 interprets it without blinking one (cybernetic) eye.

Please remember that curly braces are used in combination with placeholder or topic variables, and Whatever is used wherever without them (you might use parentheses for grouping).

Being as they are first-class citizens, how come you have only used strings and numbers as arguments, you ask? And you are right.

```
{ $_("you")}( "Hey " ~ *w )
```

In this case, you are reverting to the curly-braces version of blocks. Let's look at it from right to left: "Hey " ~ * is the argument of the function here, in parentheses because that's how blocks or functions are called. Let's go further to the left: that argument will be inserted into $_, which is the topic variable. You could go further by creating a function that returns another function, but that will have to wait until you get to the chapter on containers and you can keep things separated in different lines and statements.

Lists, Arrays, Ranges, and Sequences

Another way of aggregating data is simply arranging them together, separated by commas:

```
2, "33", { $^a + 3 }
# REPL will print:
# (2 33 -> $a { #`(Block|99905432) ... })
```

This is a List; I use a capital letter since this is one of the types in Perl 6. Elements of the lists can be of any type, including of course other lists, in which case you use the optional parentheses to group in a single element, or angular brackets if you want to make a list of strings and allomorphs without any kind of quotes:

```
(2, "33", <this is it>)
# (2 33 (this is it))
```

In the REPL response, the string quotes are suppressed, but still the nested parentheses indicate it is a list-within-a-list. For the second list, you use the quote-words quoting construct <>; you already saw it in action for defining allomorphs, but in this case it allows you to simplify the literal input of a list by eliminating commas and quotes around it. It will create a list element out of every word-like literal.

Semicolons can also be used to create lists of lists:

```
(2, "33" ; "this", "is", "it")
((2 33) (this is it))
```

Square brackets are used to refer to a particular element in a list, starting with 0:

```
(2, "33", <this is it>)[1]      # 33
(2, "33", <this is it>)[2][2] # it
```

Indexing can be used in any object that implements the Positional role.

Arrays, which can also do the Positional role, can be defined by using square brackets instead of parentheses:

```
[2, "33", <this is it>] # [2 33 (this is it)]
```

Arrays are, in fact, lists with a series of features, one of which is that they are mutable:

```
( 2, 3)[1] = 0  # Error: Cannot modify an immutable List ((2 3))
[2, 3][1] = 0   # No problem.
```

For the time being, you can then think of Arrays as mutable Lists, but you will see more differences later on.

With lists and arrays, I will introduce a new Perl 6 concept: *adverbs*, which are modifiers to operators that usually appear in postfix form, that is, after the operator. Arrays and lists use adverbs to modify the meaning of the subscript operator, the [].

```
<con cien cañones por banda>[3]:exists #True
```

These adverbs operate, in fact, on the subscript operator; thus, they can be applied to any positional data structure. The list of adverbs is shown in Table 5-1.

Table 5-1. *Positional adverbs*

Adverb	Meaning
:exists	Returns True if the subscript exists.
:k	Returns the subscript or index in the case of arrays; short for *key*, but arrays use indices or subscripts. In hashes, it returns the key.
:v	Returns the value.
:kv	Returns a list with subscript (or key) and value (in that order).
:p	Returns subscript and value as a pair.
:delete	Deletes the value at that subscript (only in arrays).

Adverbs can be negated, but it makes sense only in the first case.
:!exists will be True only if that particular subscript does not exist.

Ranges are objects that represent all the elements in a sequence whose extremes are specified. They use two dots, building a Range that goes from the one on the left to the one on the right:

```
'α'..'ω'
3.2..11.3
-3..11
```

The two extremes of the Range must be ordered; the Range will be valid but contain 0 elements if that is not the case. You can use carets to eliminate one of the extremes, or both. 3^..5 will exclude the 3, while 10..^11 will exclude the last one. Ranges are Positional objects, but one of their nice properties is that they can be used to index other Positionals; they will extract the elements that correspond to the index in the Range.

The operator minmax can also be used to generate Ranges:

```
8 minmax 3 # Range 3..8
```

It will choose the greater of the two as the highest extreme and the lesser as the lowest extreme.

If a Range starts with 0, it does not need the two periods: just a caret will do. ^3 is equivalent to 0..2 or 0..^3. This construct can be found usually as a subscript in a list or array, where Ranges are used to extract slices:

```
<con cien cañones por banda>[^3]    # con cien cañones
<con cien cañones por banda>[1..3] # cien cañones por
```

Lists of subscripts can also be used:

```
<con cien cañones por banda>[0,3]  # con por
```

And combined with Ranges, but in this case a Range will create a sublist:

```
<con cien cañones por banda>[1..2,4] # (cien cañones) banda
```

Slices also use Whatever (*) to indicate "the end of the list:"

```
<con cien cañones por banda>[*-3]    # cañones
```

Any combination of lists, Ranges, and Whatever-indexed values are obviously possible.

Whatever can also be used in another way, to define infinite Ranges:

```
'a'..* # strings that go from 'z' to 'aa'
1..Inf
300..∞
```

They are all sequences that end (or not, depending on your concept of infinity) at the infinite. Since they obviously can't be stored in non-infinite computers, they are actually examples or what are called *lazy* data structures. Lazy data structures are functional concepts, and they allow you to work within the abstract plane and operate with them without the burden of generating every single individual. In practice, components of lazy data structures are computed *only* when they are needed. If you need the nth component of a lazy data structure, you can just call it:

```
('a'..*)[301]   # kp
```

All elements up to and including the one that is called will be stored for later use.

You can operate on numeric Ranges, including infinite ones:

```
(1..*) + 3    # 4..Inf
(1..3) - 3    # -2..0
```

Table 5-2 shows the available operators for Ranges.

Table 5-2. *Select Range operators*

Operator	Operand types, left and right
+	Range, Number
+	Number, Range
-	Range, Number
*	Range, Number
*	Number, Range
/	Range, Number

The rest of the numeric operators cannot be used directly; the same goes for other non-numeric operators when the Range uses other kinds of scalars.

Sequences can be seen as more powerful Ranges and are very interesting objects. You can think of them as lists in which there is some rule that generates an element based on the previous ones. They use the ellipsis (...) or the ellipsis symbol (…).

```
33...1      # 33 to 1, counting down
1/3...9     # 0.333 to 8.333, counting up by one
'q'...'a'   # reverse alphabet, from the q to the a
```

There are several differences between Sequences and Ranges. One of the first ones is above: in Ranges, extremes are always ordered; in Sequences, they can be in any order. 'q'..'a', as a Range, would contain 0 elements.

But the other is that Sequences are actually smart objects, which are able to deduce from the first elements what is the actual sequence, as long as it is an arithmetic, that is, a sequence where every element is the previous one plus a fixed amount, or geometric, a sequence in which element is the previous one multiplied by a fixed amount:

```
(1,3.5...*)[^5]     # (1 3.5 6 8.5 11)
(2,4,8...*)[10..12] # (2048 4096 8192)
```

Arithmetic progression is assumed by default; you need three terms of the progression, as in the second example, to make Perl 6 understand this is a geometric progression. But wait, there's more!

```
(1,1, (* + *) mod 11 ... *)[32..42] # (2 3 5 8 2 10 1 0 1 1 2)
```

This is an example of the *Fibonacci modulo n* sequence. This is a *periodic* sequence, in which the patterns start to replay after a number (which is related to n). At its core is the face-like (* + *), the sum of two *, every one of them called Whatever, as you have seen before. A expression that uses Whatevers becomes, as explained in the first section of this chapter, a WhateverCode, a function which, in this case, uses Whatever to represent the previous elements in the sequence. You can use as many Whatevers as you like, with each one representing previous elements in the sequence in reverse order; namely, the first * will be the element n-1, and the second * the element n-2. In this way, you can create complex, infinite sequences, which can be applied in many different use cases, such as retry times for sending packets or simply when dealing with mathematical objects.

Not all sequences need to be infinite. You can use any expression as the right hand side of ... to indicate where it should end, like so:

```
(2,4,8 ... * > 256 ) # (2 4 8 16 32 64 128 256 512)
```

In this case, you use a WhateverCode, an expression to indicate that as soon as the number in the sequence is greater than 256, it should finish.

Hashes and Maps

Hashes and maps are two examples of classes with the Associative role. This means they are composed of key-value pairs, and in order to access the value you must have the key. The main difference between maps and hashes is the same as between lists and arrays: maps are immutable, while hashes are not. Hashes are declared using %() or curly braces:

```
%( Óðinn => "Gungnir", Þor => "Mjolnir" )
{Óðinn => Gungnir, Þor => Mjolnir}
```

There's no specific syntax for maps, so you will use a method call over a hash to create them. So

```
%( Óðinn => "Gungnir", Þor => "Mjolnir" ).Map
```

is the equivalent (immutable) map.

Maps and hashes also use curly braces for indexing:

```
%( Óðinn => "Gungnir", Þor => "Mjolnir" ).Map.{'Þor'} # Mjolnir
```

The key must be quoted, but you can eliminate quotes for keys that follow the bare identifier syntax using angular quotes:

```
{Óðinn => "Gungnir", Þor => "Mjolnir"}<Óðinn>  # Gungnir
```

In the case of hashes, this can be used to change values too:

```
{Óðinn => "Gungnir", Þor => "Mjolnir"}<Óðinn> = "Fenrir" # will
change value
```

Doing the same with maps will result in an error.

From now on, I will just use hashes as examples, with the understanding that, when reading values, maps will behave in the same way.

In the same way you did for arrays and lists, you can *slice* a hash by using a list of keys:

```
%(Freya => "Hildisvini", Odin => "Hugin",
  Thor => "Tanngniost")<Freya Thor>
# (Hildisvini Tanngniost)
```

As indicated before, <> create a list with the words within it as elements; the two values corresponding to those keys that are returned.

Adverbs mentioned in Table 5-1 can also be used in these Associatives. In this case, all :k and :kv will return the key, not the index or subscript:

```
{a => 3}<a>:k  # a
```

Also, :v can be used to extract all *existing* values in a slice:

```
say %(Freya => "Hildisvini", Odin => "Hugin",
    Thor => "Tanngniost"){"Freya","Buddy","Thor"}:v
# (Hildisvini Tanngniost)
```

The :v adverb will eliminate the non-existing elements, leaving only existing values in the resulting list; :v can be used in the same way for Positionals.

Sets, Bags, and Mixes

Sets are groups of unique objects where the order is not important. Bags are like sets, except objects can be repeated. In mixes, objects can have a fractional participation. All of them are immutable and have an equivalent with the hash suffix, which is mutable. We will use from now on the immutable versions in read-only operations, or to apply operations to pairs.

Sets might look like the kind of thing you might want to use only in math assignments. And of course, they can be used for that, but it's not the only way they can be used. Have you ever needed to find out which elements were in one group of objects and which were in the other?

That's intersection. Or the opposite—you needed to find the elements that are in one group, but not in the other; that's a set difference. You can either use another data type (such as a list) or other operations to find that out, but Perl 6 allows a very expressive way of doing the same with only one operator.

Defining a set includes the specific type you are going to define, in lowercase, followed by a list or hash, depending on the specific type:

```
set <Þor Oðinn Freya>    # set(Freya Oðinn Þor)
bag <spam spam egg spam>              # Bag(egg, spam(3))
mix { spam => 0.75, egg => 0.25}  # Mix(egg => 0.25, spam => 0.75)
```

Sets and bags take lists, while mixes take hashes or pairs. The operations these sets can be subjected to are listed in Table 5-3. All slashed versions of the operators negate the property.

Table 5-3. *Select Set, Bag, and indistinct operators*

Operators	Meaning	Works on
∈, ∉, (elem)	Belongs to (or not)	Sets and bags
∋, ∌, (cont)	Contains	Sets and bags
⊆, ⊄, (<=)	Is a subset of or equal to	Sets and bags
⊂, ⊄, (<)	Is a strict subset	Sets and bags
⊇, ⊉, (>=)	Is a superset or equal to	Sets and bags
⊃, ⊅, (>)	Strict superset	Sets and bags
∩, (&)	Intersection	All
\, (-)	Set difference	Sets and bags
⊖, (^)	Symmetric set difference	Sets and bags
∪, (|)	Union	All
⊎, (.)	Baggy multiplication	Sets and bags. Result = Bag
⊎, (+)	Baggy addition	Sets and bags. Result = Bag

These last *baggy* operations create bags out of sets of bags and deal with sets as if every individual element was an object, adding or "multiplying" them. As a matter of fact, it can take normal lists and output a bag:

```
<eggs spam> (+) <eggs spam bacon>
# Bag(bacon, eggs(2), spam(2))
```

In all these operations you can use the empty set, ∅. It will behave as a set with no elements. Multiplication or intersection with it will result in an empty set of the adequate type:

```
<eggs spam> (.) ∅  #   Bag()
```

In this case, you get an empty Bag, which is what the empty list that follows "Bag" means.

Other Data Structures

Perl 6 can also handle date and time in a native way. There are several basic data structures to do so: DateTime, Duration, and Instant.

You need two pieces of information to represent the date and time: first, the time itself and second, the time zone where that particular date and time is taking place. Together, they form the date, which can be written in one of several standard formats. The most popular one goes like this:

```
2019-02-05T19:13:38.372152Z
```

This is the actual(-ish) date I'm writing this in, and it includes a first part (before the T), with the date in the format YYYY-MM-DD, followed by the time in format hh:mm:ss.fraction

The Z indicates it is "zulu time," or UTC (universal time coordinate) time; this is actually *not* my time zone, which is more like

```
2019-02-05T20:17:39.487370+01:00
```

which indicates, at the end of the string and separated by a +/- symbol, the time difference between the Madrid time zone and UTC. Anyway, these are the standard formats that languages usually understand. Instants are actually used to represent a particular point in time. You can get the actual Instant by using the function now:

```
now # Instant:1549394401.406088
```

You can turn that Instant into a DateTime by creating one with it:

```
DateTime(now)   #2019-02-05T19:20:41.927543Z
```

Duration is used to represent lengths of time in seconds. The difference between two Instants and two DateTimes will always return a Duration:

```
now - now # -0.0014179, what it takes to process the
statements.
```

Durations can be used to compute dates in the past or future by adding or subtracting integer numbers that will be interpreted as seconds:

```
DateTime(now + 3600)   # 2019-02-05T20:24:35.224185Z
```

You can add or subtract real numbers from Durations, and you can also divide modulo a number, to find, for instance, the fraction of the hour, or day, that has passed since Instant 0:

```
now % 3600 # 1841.894321680069 (seconds from the full hour)
```

Other data structures that are used often in combination with input/output operations are buffers, called Buf in Perl 6. They are simply a series of binary elements. They are mutable and every one of the elements can be changed individually.

And here's also a new way of creating objects. Perl 6 is an object-oriented language, and thus has classes (which are kind of objects) and objects (which are particular instances of that class). You generate *new* objects of a class; many languages also use the word new for that. So a new buffer will be generated from a list of numbers via

```
Buf.new( 42, 15, 33) # Buf:0x<2A 0F 21>
```

Elements of a Buf are converted to hexadecimal when displayed. Essentially, Bufs are what you want to use if you want to work with binary data, but they are also Positional and can thus be indexed:

```
Buf:0x<2A 0F 21>[2] # 33
```

They are also, in a way, a binary representation of strings. But working with them will require a bit of what you are going to see in the next chapters.

Conclusions

You have seen how to create data and access parts of it in from the REPL. This is the same representation you will use later when building statements, so it would be great if you kept the types of data you can deal with in mind. Data can be either mutable or immutable, sometimes receiving different names depending on that. If you can access part of the data by position, it's called Positional, and if it can be accessed by key, it's Associative. Functions of all kinds are Callable.

With combinations of hashes and arrays you can create structures that are as complicated as possible and contain any kind of data. But there are other types available, used for specialized pieces of information such as dates or binary blobs of data.

You can obviously go only so far operating with *bare* data structures. You need to store them somewhere. This is where you will go in the next chapter.

CHAPTER 6

Processing Complex Data Structures

How to Transform Data in Many Different Ways

Programming is about processing data, changing and synthesizing information in many different ways. And functions are applied directly to data, which is why we will not, for the time being, deal with any way of storing that data.

Perl 6 is also object-oriented and functional. The first means that a method will be applied to data, and the way to apply it is simply by appending a period to the data structure (which might be surrounded with parentheses for convenience) and putting the name of the method behind, like so:

```
%( Óðinn => "Gungnir", Þor => "Mjolnir" ).Map
```

What you're doing is calling the method Map of the %(Óðinn => "Gungnir", Þor => "Mjolnir") hash, which is an object; this transforms the original Hash into a Map.

Let's see how the transforming functions *visit* the interior of your data structure so that Perl 6 can transform your data. But first, you need to know how to get values printed out.

© J.J. Merelo 2019
J.J. Merelo, *Perl 6 Quick Syntax Reference*, https://doi.org/10.1007/978-1-4842-4956-7_6

Different Ways of Printing

The simplest way to get something printed is to use say:

```
say 33; # outputs 33
```

But remember, in Perl 6 everything is an object. So, this is exactly the same as

```
33.say # outputs 33
```

Note that say adds a carriage return at the end of each line. If you need to output several things, you will need to put them in parentheses:

```
say( 33, 44, "Hey") # 3344Hey
```

If you want to string together several things, you can use string concatenation:

```
say( 33 ~ 44 ~ "Hey") # 3344Hey
```

But the topic variable (which you will see next), and, for that matter, any variable like the ones you will deal with in the next chapter, can be *interpolated*, that is, simply inserted inside a variable, and say will print the value:

```
$_ = 33; say("The value is $_")     # The value is 33
```

You are explicitly assigning a value to the topic variable using = above. This is not the usual way of working with it. Please check later in the chapter for a more thorough explanation of this.

Most functions use the topic variable as the default object to be applied to if no object is shown explicitly. Thus

```
$_ = 33; .say      # 33
```

and

```
$_ = 33; $_.say    # 33
```

are exactly the same.

You will need to insert say all over the place to find the result of the processing you will be doing in this chapter. Pay special attention to the last example, which will be used throughout the chapter.

Topic Variables, Their Types, and How to Generate Them

You have already seen, when dealing with blocks of code, how variable $_ appeared magically to contain data that was handed to the block as arguments. We called it the topic variable, in this case the topic scalar variable; it's accompanied by sisters the topic Positional variable @_, the topic Callable variable &_, and the topic Associative variable %_.

We can say that the parentheses we use to insert the arguments are *topicalizers*, since they *generate* a topic variable; they are your first example of this kind of thing. However, they will not be the only ones; many statements act as topicalizers, putting values into the topic variable.

The statement given acts as a simple topicalizer—nothing more and nothing less. It places whatever expression follows it into the topic variable, so that it can be used directly or indirectly via calling methods on void, like so:

```
.say given <away>          # away
given "Up" { say "You ♡" } # You ♡
given { "bar" } { .().say } # bar
```

In the first case, you are calling the .say method on void, which is equivalent to calling it on the topic variable $_, which has received its value from given. In the last case, you are using the topic Callable variable implicitly. {"bar"} creates a block (that returns "bar") and that is assigned to &_. The simple period (.) is the *method call operator*, and when followed by empty parentheses it will call the function in the implicit topic variable.

Topicalizing is useful when you want to set the *topic* to a certain object and perform several operations on it, like here:

```
say "Array has ", .elems,
    " elements which add up to ", .sum given 1..33
# Array has 33 elements which add up to 561
```

The given statement has topicalized the Range from 1 to 33 and applies two operations: .elems (which counts the number of elements of anything that looks like a list) and .sum (which adds them up). In this case, the used topic variable would have been @_. However, since you are using it implicitly (calling methods on void), that's not really seen or noticed.

While given is a pure topicalizer, with performs additional operations. This statement can be used as a suffix or prefix; it evaluates if the expression behind is defined and runs the code only if it is. But it also topicalizes.

```
.say with <this song>                    # (this song)
with Any { .say } orwith "Hey" { .say } # Hey
```

In the first case, <this song> is defined, so the statement (which in this case is in front of the condition) is run.

The output in parentheses indicates that it's printing a list. As you have seen before, angular brackets create lists, and say is able to deal with them.

In the second statement, however, Any is considered defined, which is why it runs over to the next statement. This is an object-oriented language, and it's got a whole hierarchy of classes that inherit from each other. Any is second to the top (which is Mu). All classes you have seen so far subclass Any, but it's not the kind of class you use to create objects. In this case, you are using it only as an example of undefinedness, since it's what Perl 6 understand as undefined. An object with a value is defined, even if it's empty or False. However, classes are not defined by, well, definition; they don't contain a concrete instance of an object. Any other class name would yield the same value.

This example introduces another interesting statement, orwith, which is a kind of else (for ifs) that is executed if the first condition does not hold. You can't use it as the first statement in a chain, only after a with statement.

It also uses a different form, showing how Perl 6 allows the

statement – condition – expression

```
.say - with - <this song>
```

syntax as well as

condition – expression - { statement }.

```
with - Any - { .say }
```

In this last case, the function must be explicitly shown as a block with the curly braces around it. That's the only difference, and you can choose them any way you want according to your coding standards or perceived legibility. Remember, in Perl 6 there is more than one way to do it.

There's a statement that is the opposite of with. Of course, it's called without:

```
say "With or" without Mu  # With or
```

Mu is the class that is at the top of the hierarchy; it's the topmost class from where all other classes inherit. That does not matter, however; it's simply a class and thus it's not defined, so `without` runs the statement to its left.

The `andthen` operator is equivalent to `with`, except it only works as a suffix:

```
"Away from Toronto" andthen .say  # Away from Toronto
```

Its behavior if it's not defined is slightly different. Instead of not running the code or going to the next `without` statement, it will return an empty list, so

```
Any andthen .say
```

will not print anything, but it's actually an empty list.

Actually, an empty `Slip`. More about this later.

Basic Object Methods and How to Call Them

The summit of the Perl 6 class hierarchy is `Mu`. `Mu` hosts methods that are available throughout the whole class hierarchy; all regular objects you will find are an instance of `Mu`. That is why it's interesting to know a few methods that you might need to use. They are in Table 6-1. Please see the "First Responders" section from Chapter 2 for the whole list.

Table 6-1. *Select Mu methods*

Method	Description
defined	Returns True if it's a *type* object, False if it's a class.
isa	True if the object belongs to that class or a subclass.
does	True if the object is exactly of that class.
gist	Returns a representation of the object; is called on an object by say.
perl	Returns the object in a way that can be evaluated to reproduce the object.
so	Converts to a Boolean value corresponding to the object value.
not	As above, but negates the value.
print	Converts to a string and ouputs the value.
put	Prints and adds a new line at the end.

These methods are available all across all objects of all classes you have seen so far.

```
42.defined.say      # True
<1 2 3>.print       # 1 2 3
<1 2 3>.gist.print  # (1 2 3) (same as <1 2 3>.say)
0.so.put            # False
1.not.put           # False
```

As you can see above, since the application of a method also returns an object, this object can be applied to a method too. 42.defined returns a Boolean, which can be say-ed or print-ed as shown in every example. In Perl, there are always many ways to do something, and some of these methods can also be used as simple routines, preceding the arguments, like so:

```
put not 1    # False, same as 1.not.put
```

You don't need to use the parentheses for function calls unless there could be some ambiguity:

```
say not 1, 2              # False2
```

The "," is interpreted as separating two items that are going to be printed, so you have to use

```
say(not((1, 2)))
```

instead. Since not as a routine takes a single argument, you have to put parentheses around (1,2) to make it a single object; the second set of parentheses apply the not routine to it, and eventually the result gets passed to say.

This is a lot of parentheses indeed. This is why in most cases the object.method syntax is preferred.

Next up the hierarchy is the Any class, which, as its name implies, is inherited by almost any class in the Perl 6 class hierarchy.

As a matter of fact, its only sibling is Junction. More on this later.

Any is not intended to be instantiated, but it includes many methods that are used by subclasses. In general, these methods assume there's some internal structure there. Table 6-2 shows just a few of them, the most widely used ones.

Table 6-2. *Most frequent methods of the class Any*

Method	Description
elems	Returns the number of elements
min	Returns the smallest element (in a numeric sense)
max	Returns the largest one
minmax	Returns a Range bookended by the smallest and largest
keys	Returns the keys, which are indices if it's a Positional
values	Returns the list of the values, which is equivalent to the list itself for lists, and the values in hashes.
unique	Returns every element a single time
repeated	Returns only elements that appear more than once
squish	Returns only the last element of sequences which repeat the same one

Since these methods belong to Any, they can be used by Positional and Associative, as well as simple scalars (most of these will return a trivial value, though), like so:

```
("þ" xx 3, "ð" xx 4, "ß" xx 5).Mix.elems.say  # 3
say 3.elems              # 1
say (5,7,-3,2).minmax  # -3..7
```

You will use these functions throughout the rest of the chapter and the book, so please keep them in mind; in general, they do what they mean and the name is similar to the one used in other languages (except for elems, which will usually be called length or size; elems, as in elements, is much more informative, though).

Perl 6 is the opposite of a minimalist language. It was not created to be memorized, because there are lots of different functions and options. Just get the general idea of what you can do with an object and its syntax, and a search engine will be your friend to grab the actual way of saying something.

Processing Data in a Functional Way

You have already checked out one of the tenets of functional programming: functions as first-class citizens. Let's get to another: processing using functions rather than looping constructs. As a matter of fact, and quite purposefully, this goes first in the book. In general, using functions to process data structures will be more efficient and closer to how you would express your intention mathematically. That is, if you want to apply function f to object x, which is a list, it's better to express it as f(x) or as x.f (in object form) than as a loop, which says first take the first number from the list x, then apply f to the first element, then to the second, and so on. Get used to thinking functionally and your programs will be much more expressive and also faster.

This is why the first function you will see is a function that applies another function to any data structure and is called map. This is not a map of the kind you see in atlases, but a mathematical map, that is, an application f that takes a as input and gives b as an output: f: a → b.

```
say (1..5).map: ( 0x2134 + * ).chr # (א ב ג ד i)
```

This maps a list that goes from 0 to 5 to the first letters of the Hebrew alphabet. You are also using here a new way of passing arguments to a function: a colon is used to separate map from the arguments it's using. In this case it's totally equivalent to using paired parentheses, only it saves a character and makes it cleaner. There is an alternative syntax for map.

It's a routine form of map that takes the object as the second argument, as shown:

```
say map ( 0x2134 + * ).chr, 1..5   # (א ב ג ד i)
```

In this case, the parentheses are also optional. The routine form of object methods always takes the object as the second argument, conventionally.

As shown above by the parentheses, map returns a Sequence whatever it's taking as an input, be it a list, a Range (as in this case), or another sequence. But this is a good thing. Remember infinite sequences? They can also be mapped... to the infinite and beyond:

```
say (1,1, * + * ... *).map: *² #   (...)
```

That ellipsis among parentheses is the way Perl 6 say, "Well, this thing is big. Let's take a slice." So

```
say ((1,1, * + * ... *).map: *²)[1000..^1005]
```

will print a humongous amount of numbers, which are the 1000th to the 1004th elements in the squared Fibonacci sequence. As seen in their chapter, lazy sequences compute their elements only when they are needed, which is what they do in this case.

Some other functions also map from one domain to another, but what you want to know is which elements meet a condition. Grep, as in the Linux command-line utility grep, will help you with that.

Curious about knowing the first elements of the Fibonacci sequence that are divisible by 3?

```
say ((1,1, * + * ... *).grep: * %% 3)[^5]    # (3 21 144 987 676 )
```

grep will only return those elements of the object that will make the expression be True; the rest will be dropped. 3 and 21 are obviously divisible by 3, so they are included in the output. The rest between them are skipped.

This is also a Sequence, as in the case of map; this means you can chain map and grep:

```
say (1,1, * + * ... *).grep( * %% 3 ).map( *² )[10..14]
# (491974210728665289 23112315624967704576
1085786860162753449801
# 51008870112024444436089  2396331108404986135046400)
```

You can do this as much as you want, mapping a to b and filtering it to c and back again to mapping and filtering.

And of course, if there's a map, there's a reduce.

MapReduce is a thing and the name of a framework you can use for big data processing; map and reduce are pairs of functions usually found in any functional language.

Note that reduce applies a function to a whole list by applying it to the first two elements, and then recursively to the result of this and the next element, eventually yielding a single result. It's thus a binary function or a function with two arguments; it could be an infix operator. Unsurprisingly, a method called reduce is used for this purpose.

Let's compute, for instance, the product of the first terms of the Fibonacci sequence:

```
say (1,1, * + * ... * > 10000).reduce: * * *
#   1060994397609463450470261049385958297600000
```

This expression has a profusion of asterisks; all but one are examples of Whatever. That one is simply the product symbol; it's the next-to-last one. You have created a Fibonacci sequence that stops when one term is greater than 10000, thus having just a few terms. You need the sequence to be finite, because reduce is not going to act on lazy data structures. The function you are applying is behind the colon, and it goes like this (you probably guessed it already): the first asterisk is the result of the reduction so far, the second is the product, and the third is the value of the current element. This example shows how it works:

```
say (1..10).reduce: * ~ "→" ~ *
# 1→2→3→4→5→6→7→8→9→10
```

The leftmost `Whatever` will receive the result so far and the second-from-last the current element. You might not want to stick to the order in which the elements arrive; use the placeholders you saw in previous chapters:

```
say (1..10).reduce: { $^b ~ "→" ~ $^a }
# 10→9→8→7→6→5→4→3→2→1
```

`Whatever` turns the expression it's in, in the adequate context, into code, magically surrounding it with curly braces, as you saw in the previous example. That is not the case with these placeholders: they are only understood if they are placed in a code block, surrounded by curly braces. On the other hand, they receive the arguments *in alphabetical order*. The first argument (result so far) will go to the first in alphabetical order, which is $^a in this case, and so on. Therefore, in this case, the sequence is inverted.

An alternative way to use the reduce operation is to use *metaoperators*. Metaoperators surround binary infix operators with square brackets to imply that they are actually used as *reduce* operators, that is, applied to the first and second, then to the result and third, and so on:

```
say [*] 1..13 # 6227020800
```

This is actually 13!, or the factorial of 13, the product of all numbers from 13 down to 1. The infix operator ∗ is surrounded by [ ] to convert it into a reduce operator. And this is not limited to numbers:

```
say [~] <a b c d>  # abcd
```

You might need to know the partial results and generate a list with them. The so-called triangular-reduction metaoperator does just that:

```
[\~] <a b c d>   # (a ab abc abcd)
```

Reduction operators always return Sequences, and they can be lazy (or infinite, depending on how you look at them). Applying them to a lazy sequence will result in another lazy sequence, which will have your result ready just when you need it. For instance,

```
say ([\*] 1..*)[31] # 263130836933693530167218012160000000
```

This is a perfect example of how Perl 6 saves you a lot of coding, and how complicated loops in other languages can be reduced to a single line. But there are loops too.

All functional operations can be chained together, since they return a value:

```
say (1,1, * + * ... * > 10000).map( *² ).grep( * %% 2 ).reduce
( * + * )
# 126886032
```

You apply map to the sequence, which returns another sequence, to which you apply grep, filtering out only the even values, and eventually reduce to the result of that, yielding the result.

But this can be expressed in a different way using the *feed or rocket* operator ==>, like so:

$$\text{say} (1,1, *+* ... *> 10000 ==> \text{map}(*^2) ==>$$
$$\text{grep}(* \%\% 2) ==> \text{reduce}(*+*))$$

Syntactically, what this operator does is to take the operand on the left-hand side and use it as the second argument to the routine on the right-hand side. Remember that all of these functions have a method and a routine form. So the first application of the rocket operator is actually equal to

$$\text{map}(*^2, (1,1, *+* ... *> 10000))$$

which is clearly much less visually clear. You could apply `.grep` to this, or wrap it again in a routine-type call to `grep` and so on. All three syntaxes (method, feed operator, routine) are possible in Perl 6, so you just choose the one that feels more legible to you or your coworkers.

Vector Operators and Meta-Operators

Several operators perform operations on lists, resulting in other lists. See Table 6-3.

Table 6-3. *X and Z list operators*

Operator	Action
X	*Vectorial* multiplication. Creates a list of pairs of every element in the left with every element in the right.
Z	*Zip* operator. Creates a list of pairs with elements on the left and the corresponding element on the right.

They can operate on lists of different length:

```
say ^2 X 3..5  #((0 3) (0 4) (0 5) (1 3) (1 4) (1 5))
```

But Z will cut to the shortest length:

```
say ^2 Z 3..5 # ((0 3) (1 4))
```

They are extremely convenient as meta-operators. Simply append the binary operator you want to apply to every one of the resulting pairs:

```
say 10..12 X** 3..5
# (1000 10000 100000 1331 14641 161051 1728 20736 248832)
<J Q K Ace> X~ <♣ ♦ ♥ ♠>
# (J♣ J♦ J♥ J♠ Q♣ Q♦ Q♥ Q♠ K♣ K♦ K♥ K♠ Ace♣ Ace♦ Ace♥ Ace♠)
```

In the first case, ** (raised to) is the operator that is applied to the pairs; in the second, it's the string concatenation operator ~.

Loops

In Perl 6, loop control structures are keywords, that is, they are purely syntax interpreted by the language, not functions defined as part of the object system. This allows greater flexibility in handling the way they are employed and more efficiency when running them, since they are recognized explicitly and immediately. There are many different loop constructs, differing on whether they return value or not their termination conditions, and how they generate the next iteration. I'll try to summarize in Table 6-4.

Table 6-4. *Features of loops*

Keyword	Topic	Termination	Next iteration	Returns value
for	✓	IterationEnd	Iteration.pull-one	✓
loop	✗	Condition in ternary expression	Increment in ternary expression	✓
while, until	✗	Expression	Internal	✗
repeat	✗	Expression	Internal	✗
do	✗	Runs once	N/A	✓

The for keyword is the workhorse of loops, and it is used to iterate over data structures that admit it. These data structures have the Iterable role. All Positional and Associative data structures you know have that role, so you can work with them. But what for does is to call .iterator on that data structure. For every iteration it will call pull-one on the resulting iterator, and compare this to the constant `IterationEnd` to find out if it's finished. In general, this is transparent to the user, since Perl 6 will take care of generating sensible values for every data structure:

```
.say for %( :a, :b, :c )   # c => True b => True a => True
.say for <a b c>           # a b c »
.say for set <a b c>    # a => True b => True c => True
```

In all cases above, you are using the implicit topic variable. You are also using for as a suffix, which is convenient if there's a single statement inside the loop, thus saving the curly braces:

```
for set <a b c> { say $_.value??$_.key!!"" }; # «b a c »
```

The explicit topic variable $_ will be of type Pair. You will just print the key, which is the element in the set; you do that in the block.

But you can explicitly declare a variable; that variable can be anything you want depending on what the iterator is going to return every turn. In this case, the result of the vectorial operation X is going to be a list with two elements:

```
for 1..3 X <A B C> -> @pair {
    say (@pair[0] == 1)??~@pair!! ~@pair ~ "s"
} # 1 A 1 B 1 C 2 As 2 Bs 2 Cs 3 As 3 Bs 3 Cs
```

This is useful in this case, where you want that fact to be featured quite legibly in your code.

But remember that in Perl 6 there is always more than one way to do something, and you could use the implicit @_ for concision if you had wanted.

Since for is one of the loop structures that returns values, you can leave the printing for when the loop has finished, or use a single say statement in front of the loop:

```
say (for 1..3 X <A B C> -> @pair { (@pair[0] == 1)??~@pair!! ~@
pair ~ "s" })
# (1 A 1 B 1 C 2 As 2 Bs 2 Cs 3 As 3 Bs 3 Cs)
```

You need to surround for with parentheses to capture the output, which will be a list, as denoted by the parentheses around it.

The loop statement also produces a result, and it can be used either with a C-style triplet of statements: one for variable declaration, the next for checking for termination, and the last for incrementing the value:

```
say (loop (my $i = 3; $i < 200 ; $i*=3 ) { $i² })
# (9 81 729 6561)
```

The statement do is barely a loop, since it simply gathers the output of an expression so that it can be assigned to a variable or simply captured. It can be a way of capturing complex expressions within statements that would not allow them.

The while and repeat statements behave in a slightly different way, mainly with respect to checking the condition for termination:

```
$_ = 3; repeat {  $_*=3; say $_² } until $_ > 20;
$_ = 3; while $_ <= 20 {  $_*=3; say $_² }
```

These two loops will print 81 and 729 and will run the same number of times. However, repeat loops will iterate at least once; while loops might not even run once if the condition is not met.

As conditions, while and until are the opposite of each other but can be used in the same conditions: you can end a repeat loop with while, or have an until loop, which will iterate until the condition is met.

There are several commands that work only inside loops and are independent of the loop construct available. The next command will skip the rest of the iteration and start the next one:

```
$_ = 1; until $_ > 200 { $_*=3; next if $_.comb.elems == 2; say
$_² }
# 9
# 81
# 59049
```

This loop will skip all multiples of 3 that have 2 figures (the number –elems– of elements –comb-- in the string is equal to 2), producing the squares of only those that have a single figure like 3 or 9 or 3 like 243.

Another such command is last, which will exit a loop. It can be used together with the loop keyword and without any kind of loop variable to exit when it's needed:

```
$_ = 3; loop {  $_*=3; say $_²; last if $_ > 20 }
# 81
# 729
```

Decisions

One of the easiest ways to make a decision is to use the ternary operator. This operator checks the value of an expression, and it returns the first result if it's true and the second if it's false. In most languages it uses ? and : as the operators separating the expression from true-result and a true from a false result. Perl 6 uses ?? and !! (or their Unicode, single grapheme equivalent, ?? and ‼):

```
say (max 1,7 ... * > 30) < 34 ?? "Smaller" !! "Greater"   #
Smaller
```

You might wonder if the first number in that sequence that is greater than 30 is smaller than 34. It happens to be 31, so it's smaller and the first result is returned.

But throughout hundreds of computer languages, if has been consecrated as the decision-making statement par excellence. You can use it in the traditional way, preceding the condition, or behind the condition, as here:

```
say "Smaller" if (max 1,7 ... * > 30)  < 34 # Smaller
```

You miss the other part, of course, the one that will do something if the condition is false. You already saw that with can do that, together with orwith. But that requires another condition, so let's introduce the well-known statement else:

```
if (max 1,7 ... * > 30)  < 34 { say "Smaller"} else { say
"Greater"}
# Smaller
```

Since Perl 6 uses curly braces for separating blocks, you can fit everything in a single line. Use if instead of the ternary operator if the operations you need to perform depending on the result of the expression exceed returning a single value; if will also act as a block, returning a value. This example shows it in combination with elseif, which will run if the previous expression is False but perform an additional operation:

```
say (if M > 1000 { ">1k" } elsif  M == 1000 { "1k" } else {
"<1k" }) # 1k
```

You enclose the whole block in parentheses to pass the result to say.

The opposite of if is unless, which will run the block (or return the last element in the block) only if the result of the expression is false:

```
say "Not eight" unless 7 == VII # OUTPUT: «Not eight »
```

The with statement can also be used, but only when you want to test for definedness. There is also a way of testing different values using given, which I have referred to before:

```
given M cmp 1000 { when More {say "M"}; when Same {say "S"};
default {say "L"} } # S
```

The given statement topicalizes the result of the expression and when tests for the value, which would be in the topic variable, which is implicit. In this case, it will print "S" since M is the Roman numeral for 1,000.

Conclusions

In this chapter, you have focused on single line, *reactive* functions that take on data structures to produce a result. This is the foundation for all programs, which are basically processes that transform data structures. However, working with single data structures, without storing the result anywhere, only takes you so far. You will need work with *data containers*, which is what you will tackle in the next chapter.

CHAPTER 7

Storing Data: Containers

How to Store Data into Variables, Specify Where Those Containers Can Be Seen, and How They Can Change or Be Destructured

When learning the syntax of a new programming language it's important to understand every piece of what's going on separately: how you write different types, what functions are available to process them, and how you make decisions in a program. These actions work literally by analyzing and acting on every character of every line and every statement created by those characters.

So far, you have worked with statements that can be written in a single line, either in the REPL or in one of the online services mentioned in Chapter 1. You are going to work, from this chapter onwards, on full scripts that you might want to edit using a programming editor and store locally. Let's see what a full Perl 6 script looks like:

```
#!/usr/bin/env perl6

use v6;

given M cmp 1000 {
    when More {say "M"}
```

© J.J. Merelo 2019

J.J. Merelo, *Perl 6 Quick Syntax Reference*, https://doi.org/10.1007/978-1-4842-4956-7_7

```
    when Same {say "S"}
    default {say "L"}
}
```

The output of this file should be "S", the same as the single-line statements you saw in the last chapter. There are several changes with respect to the version shown in the previous chapter:

- The *shebang* line has been added to the beginning of the file. This line has three parts. The first is the shebang herself, #!, which indicates to the shell that what follows is a program that needs to be loaded to interpret the rest of the file. The second part is /usr/bin/env, which indicates that, instead of hard-wiring the location of the interpreter, you should look for it in the environment, that is, looking at the command interpreter variable tells you where you should look for runnable programs. This is needed for several reasons, including the fact that version managers like rakudobrew (mentioned in Chapter 1) change the path to the Perl 6 binary. The perl6 that follows it indicates the name of the interpreter; this line is equivalent to running which perl6 in the command line, that is, it will return the actual path to the interpreter, although env also loads it. OSX users will use it anyway, and it will not hurt in Windows, although it's not really used. The objective of this shebang line is to be able to run the script by just issuing the file name.

- The use v6 line is included. This is a pragma, which is an instruction that tells the interpreter how to deal with the rest of the file, but it's addressed not to the Perl 6 interpreter, but to Perl 5, which will issue an error if it sees it, something like this:

```
Perl v6.0.0 required--this is only v5.20.0, stopped at
given.p6 line 3.
```

- When spreading the sentences to different lines, the semicolons at the end of the line have been dropped. Perl 6 always finishes its sentences with semicolons, except when there is a curly brace closing at the end of the line. That is why it is not needed in these cases.

You need to run this file now, which I have called given.p6.

You can find all scripts from this chapter on in the repository at https://github.com/JJ/perl6-quick-reference-apress under a directory appropriately named with the chapter number and on the Apress site for this book.

Using perl6 given.p6 will work everywhere if perl6 is installed correctly. If you are using Windows, writing given.p6 should also work. If you are using Linux, BSD, or OSx, you need to issue a chmod +x given.p6 to make it executable and then run ./given.p6.

So now you can create and run your own programs. And programs keep state in several places. Let's learn about this next.

Where a Container Resides: Scope

First, let's see if we are on the same page here. I am going to talk about what is called a *variable* everywhere. However, this is a loaded word that implies, for instance, that it might *vary*. This may or may not be the case in Perl 6, so I prefer to talk about *containers*. Containers store values and have a series of additional properties. Besides, this name also decouples the container from its content. Variables are more like a tag or label you slap on a piece of data. Containers have actual agency, and they store data, but some other operations can be performed on them too, even if they are not associated with any piece of data.

The first thing containers have is a *name* which follows the *bare identifier* syntax, which I mentioned in Chapter 3 when talking about pairs and again in Chapter 5 when mentioning the names of placeholders with twigils.

There is also an extended syntax for identifiers. This will be explained later in the chapter.

As a reminder, they have to start with a letter or underscore and can be followed by letters, underscores, apostrophes, dashes, and numbers (these last ones as long as they are not preceded by a dash, and terminated by letters, underscores, or numbers). The following are all valid identifier names:

```
first-class
secondary
chapter1
Chapter_2
_cool_
it's-here
```

In most cases, container names are preceded by a sigil, which is related to the default role the data they contain is going to have. These sigils are shown in Table 7-1.

Table 7-1. *Sigils*

Sigil	Default role
$	Scalar
@	Positional
%	Associative
&	Callable

Thus, `$chapter1` will by default contain a scalar, `@secondary` will contain data with the Positional role, such as a list or array, and `%_cool_` will contain an Associative value. Of course, `&first-class` will contain a Callable.

Sigil-less containers can also be used, but let's leave them for a bit later.

This might imply some kind of *coercion* when one data type is assigned to a container:

```
my $var = 3; say $var   # 3
my @var = 3; say @var   # [3]
```

Same data. However, in the second case, since it's assigned to a Positional, it's effectively turned into an array.

```
my @var = :a; say @var   # [a => True]
my %var = :a; say %var   # {a => True}
```

The same pair becomes either a single-element array that contains a pair, or a hash with a single key, depending on the sigil the container uses:

```
(my @var=1,2).say # [1 2]
(my %var=1,2).say  # {1 => 2}
```

In this case, a list assigned to a @-sigilled or a %-sigilled variable will become either a two-element array or a hash whose key is the first element. Trying the same with a list with an odd number of elements will fail, as should be expected. Please see also this way of working: you are surrounding the variable declaration with parentheses. An important thing you should remember about Perl 6 is that it's a strangely consistent language. Parentheses are not just syntax; they create a list and that list can be printed with say, as shown here. Parentheses, however, do not create a scope by themselves. That variable will be available outside the parentheses once it's been declared.

The next required attribute in a container is the *scope*. The scope indicates where the container should be visible or accessible. And *my* indicates block scope, that is, it's limited by the curly braces around it; the variable will not be seen outside the block where it's been declared. This is called *lexical* scope.

Let's rewrite the program in the first section to use a scoped variable:

```
my $is-it-K = M cmp 1000;
given $is-it-K {
    when More {say "M"}
    when Same {say "S"}
    default {say "L"}
}
```

The $is-it-K variable (which can also use capitals; K here is used to represent 1K as in 1,000) is going to contain a scalar value. You don't care about the actual type of the contained data; in this case, it's going to be a Bool, but the variable could hold anything.

You are using = for assignment. Once a variable is declared, it can be used and get a new value, even if it's a different type:

```
my $is-it-K = M cmp 1000;
my $result = ( given $is-it-K {
                    when More {"M"}
                    when Same {"S"}
                    default {"L"}
            }
        );
$is-it-K = "Yes" if $result eq "S";
say $is-it-K;
```

This will print "Yes", the value of $is-it-K, which has changed from Bool to Str without a problem. The new code also shows how to make a statement like given return a value that is going to be stored in $result. As is usual in blocks, this statement will return the value of the last instruction executed, which in this case is going to be the "S" string. In general, it's a good practice for a function or expression to return a value instead of taking any kind of action with it (like using say) which the user might or might not want. That is what you do here.

However, that actually looks like a function. And functions are first-class citizens in Perl 6. So, let's store them somewhere and use them from there:

```
my $is-it-K = -> $test { given $test {
                    when More {"M"}
                    when Same {"S"}
                    default {"L"}
            }
        };

say $is-it-K(M cmp 1000) eq "S" ?? "Yes" !! "No";
```

The result is exactly the same, but you have used the *pointy block* syntax to declare a block; this block will use the variable (or variables) declared behind the "pointy" part, the →, instead of the placeholders that you have used so far. The block will return the value returned by the last statement. Once declared, a block, pointy or not, is kind of like a scalar, so it can be held in a scalar container. It's a good occasion to introduce the ampersand sigil:

```
my &is-it-K = -> $test { given $test {
                             when More {"M"}
                             when Same {"S"}
                             default {"L"}
              }
          };
say is-it-K(M cmp 1000) eq "S" ?? "Yes" !! "No";
```

When you declare a variable (which is what you do when you create a container) using an ampersand, you are saying that it is going to be a function. So you can just skip the ampersand if you want and call it the usual way you do with functions, just using the function name.

Come this point, you may have realized that what the function does is to convert the result of a test into a string, so the name you gave it might be a bit unfair. Plus it's a full-fledged function, so you might as well declare it as such:

```
sub cmp-to-s( $lhs, $rhs ) {
    given $lhs cmp $rhs {
        when More {"M"}
        when Same {"S"}
        default {"L"}
    }
}

say cmp-to-s(M, 1000) eq "S" ?? "Yes" !! "No";
```

Routines are declared with the sub keyword and are variables just like any other. They also return, by default, the value returned by the last statement. But unlike blocks, you can actually use a return statement to explicitly state what you are returning. You can assign the result to a variable and return that variable, which will help you debug it if needed:

```
sub cmp-to-s( $lhs, $rhs ) {
    my $result = ( given $lhs cmp $rhs {
        when More {"M"}
        when Same {"S"}
        default {"L"}
    });
    return $result;
}

say cmp-to-s(M, 1001) eq "S" ?? "Yes" !! "No";
```

You have surrounded the given statement with parentheses, which act, in this case, as an evaluator. Not using them would be syntactically incorrect, since it would be using a block within a simple assignment.

You don't need to, but can if you want, declare a scope for them; a lexical scope (my) is assumed. The & sigil, in this case as above, plays a role, and it's to distinguish between the container (which holds the function code) from the contained (which is the function itself). You use the sigil when you want to retrieve the value of the container; you drop the sigil when you want to use the value of the container:

```
sub hello() {  "Hello"; }
my $hello = hello; # Will contain "Hello"
my &copy-of-hello = &hello; # Will contain a copy of the function
say "Original ", $hello, " and copy ", copy-of-hello;
```

In this case, you use a variable to *contain* the result of a routine and the sigilled version to indicate the routine itself. You obtain the value of the former and you call the latter, which obviously returns the same value.

The scope of a variable can also be temporal, or temp. These variables have block scope but *inherit* the value of the outer scope:

```
my $us-fugit = now;

sub this-will-take( $n ) {
    temp $us-fugit;
    my @fib = 1,1, * + * ... ∞;
    my $nth = @fib[$n];
    (my $save, $us-fugit) = ($us-fugit, now);
    return $nth, $us-fugit - $save, $us-fugit;
}

for 100,1000,10000 {
    my ($res,$took,$final ) = this-will-take( $_ );
    say "Computing $res took $took from start finished at
$final";
}
say "Everything took ", now - $us-fugit;
```

You are using the same variable name, $us-fugit, to measure time outside *and* inside the this-will-take routine; it will be used to keep the time it took and also when it finished. $us-fugit is initialized with the value *outside* the routine, and it's reassigned by the end of the routine. You are using an array assignment here: the left-hand side of (my $save, $us-fugit) = ($us-fugit, now); declares $save and also uses $us-fugit, already declared, and you assign them in exactly the same order. You use a similar technique in the first line in the loop that declares the three variables. Note that, in this case, my is outside the parentheses, meaning that you declare the scope of all three variables whose value will be returned by the routine. Note that return in this-will-take effectively returns a list and its values will be assigned to those three variables in turn.

State variables, on the other hand, keep the value from one invocation to the next and are initialized just once:

```
sub this-will-take( $n ) {
    state $us-fugit = now;
    my @fib = 1,1, * + * ... ∞;
    my $nth = @fib[$n];
    (my $save, $us-fugit) = ($us-fugit, now);
    return $nth, $us-fugit - $save, $us-fugit;
}

for 100,1000,10000 {
    my ($res,$took,$final ) = this-will-take( $_ );
    say "Computing $res took $took, finished at $final";
}
```

I have typeset in boldface the main change (from the previous example). Two lines have also been eliminated. $us-fugit is initialized when the subroutine is invoked for the first time, and from then on it keeps the value so that you will measure the time it takes from an instant before the value of the previous invocation was returned.

Additionally, you can hide variables from lexical scope using anon.

Classes and How to Identify Them

Perl 6 uses *duck typing*, with certain restrictions: it assigns a class to a literal, and then to the container that holds it, depending on what it looks like. But you can also constrain what a container might hold by using type constraints, which go between the scope and the variable name declaration, so

```
my Int @array= 1,2,3
```

will be exclusively composed of Ints and the program will fail if you try to assign something else to an element. You can obviously constrain the value of scalars:

```
my Str $name = "Þor"
```

In the case of hashes, there are two values involved: keys and values. Using the same syntax as above will restrict the *value* types:

```
my Int %hash = %( 'eggs' => 3, 'zucchini' => 2 )
```

But you can restrict both:

```
my Int %hash{Bool};
%hash{True} = 3;
```

The class between the curly braces will restrict the type of keys, which in this case must be Bool, and the class preceding the variable name will restrict the values.

This also illustrates the fact that containers are instances of a class, that is, a meta-level class that produces, effectively, containers with a certain class. Perl 6 includes a meta-object protocol which makes it easy to create new types from scratch, but also to *introspect* or ask about some aspects of some piece of data, including a container. It even has a special syntax to access the methods of the metaclass: a caret, ^. When you find one, it means "this method is not from the class, it's from the metaclass." In this chapter, we are mainly interested in classes and types. You can use ^name to interrogate the metaclass about what kind of class the container belongs to:

```
say {3}.^name; # Block
say (my @a).^name # Array
```

Please check how, in this case, you have defined a container on the fly by giving it a scope and then examining it. Also, in this case, it shows how defining a variable as a Positional (with the @ sigil) will give it, by default, the Array class, which is the simplest Positional mutable class.

The meta-object protocol goes much further than that. You can modify, for instance, attributes in real time. I will introduce more syntax in the chapter devoted to classes.

Other meta-object methods might be useful:

```
3.^methods.say
# Returns usable methods: new Capture Int Num Rat
Str.^mro.say
# Ordered class hierarchy: ((Str) (Cool) (Any) (Mu))
```

Assignment, Coercion, Mutability, and Binding

Containers need to contain. This is why they were created; this is what they are for. However, there are different ways of containing, and different ways of finding out what's contained and changing it. The first thing that should be clear is that the container and containee might have a different class:

```
my @a = 1,2,3;
say @a.^name;      # Array
say (1,2,3).^name # List
```

Containers will behave as the closest class to the original that's mutable. In some cases, you might need the container to behave exactly like you want it to; you use *binding* in that case:

```
my @a := 1,2,3;
say @a.^name;      # List
```

In this case, @a will *bind* to the list and thus will behave exactly like that list, class equal to List and all. Binding, however, also implies something else: although it keeps being a container, their destinies will be bound unless it's bound to something else. In this, any assignment to @a will fail (since a List is immutable). However,

```
@a := 4,5;
```

will rebind @a to another List and is perfectly acceptable. Binding to an immutable value is not the most common use of binding. Actually, creating aliases for containers is also a use case:

```
my @to-be-bound = <a b c>;
my @binder := @to-be-bound;
say @binder;
@to-be-bound[1] = 'þ';
say @binder; # [a þ c]
@binder[1] = 'p';
say @to-be-bound; # [a p c]
```

The two variables are bound to each other and are actually the same.

On the other hand, there are actual constants in Perl 6. They are assigned once—in fact, during compilation time. They will never change.

```
constant %what = { doesn't => 'change' };
# {doesn't => change}
```

Perl 6 will complain if you try to change that value, making that container immutable. Some data structures are also immutable, and that is inherited by the containers as long as you are trying to modify the contained data, not the contained value.

Sigilless variables are a special case. For starters, they don't have a default type, so they can be used for any kind of data. But the main difference is that they act as an alias for the data they are assigned and thus are also *bound* to that specific piece of data, like so:

```
my @de-sigilled = ^3;
(my \up-to-three = @de-sigilled).say;
@de-sigilled[3] = 3;
up-to-three.say;
up-to-three[4] = 4;
say @de-sigilled; # [0 1 2 3 4]
```

The scope declaration of sigilless variables uses an escape character to avoid confusion; this is no longer used when it's employed later on. Here you see how (the increasingly inaccurately described) up-to-three is bound to @de-sigilled and you can use one or the other to change data. In this case, you use the simple mechanism of indexing past the (original) end to extend the array until it contains 0 to 4.

Constants are also the mechanism used to define special numbers in the language core. As long as Perl 6 has full Unicode support, it could just as well include some numbers that have traditionally been represented by a letter or combination of letters. They are shown in Table 7-2.

Table 7-2. *Unicode symbols for mathematical constants used in Perl 6*

Number	Value/Explanation
pi, π	3.141592653589793
tau, τ	$2*\pi$,6.283185307179586
e, *e*	Euler's constant, 2.718281828459045

Contexts

Context is a mechanism used by Perl 6 to call specific methods on a variable to make it behave properly when asked to be something else. The simplest example of this is when you need to print the contents of a variable; that variable needs to be in *string* context because it's going to be visualized as such. But not only: some operators force a numeric context, for instance.

But one context you will find often in Perl 6 is called a *sink* context. It's invoked when no one is there to use the value returned by an operation. In general, it's not something you will want to put your objects on, but a kind of error that will arise with a certain frequency if you don't pick up the value yielded by a routine.

For some other context, Table 7-3 shows the *contextualizer* operator (that is, the one that will be applied to the object to put it in that object) and also the function that will be called on the object in order to do that.

Table 7-3. *Contexts, their operators, and the method they call on objects coerced to them*

Context	Contextualizer	Method
Sink	(Not using value)	`sink-all` (for Seqs)
Number	Arithmetic operators (+, -, *, /)	`Numeric`
String	~, also put	`Str`
Item	$	`item`
List	, and @	`list`

Maybe we need to pay attention to the last two elements of the list. The comma is the list contextualizer in the sense that it will *listify* whatever lies to its left-hand side and combine it with whatever is on its right-hand side. Assigning to a Positional container will also create a list by itself, as you have seen:

```
say (3,).^name;
say (3, my @ = 2,3,4).^name;
```

These two are lists, in the first case with a single element, in the second case a nested list with two elements. In this second case, you have created an anonymous Positional consisting of just a sigil; since you are defining it this way simply for grouping the numbers and also putting them in list context (you could have use a parenthesis) you don't need to give it a name. This variable is also a *state* variable in the sense mentioned before, so it can be used as such without the need to declare it.

But @ is also a list context operator in another sense, combined with the previous operator. The item is equivalent to a scalar context. An object in a scalar or item context will seem to have no internal structure and behave as a single entity:

```
(my $itemized = $[1,2,3]).perl.put; # $[1,2,3]
$itemized[2].say; # 3
@$itemized.perl.put;
```

You are first itemizing an array by putting $ in front. That way, you can assign it to a scalar and also use it a Positional, as shown in the second statement. You are using `.perl` here, which is a *machine-readable* representation of the data structure. In this case, it's printing the data structure with a $ in front, so as to say, "Hey, this is actually a single item."

In the last line of the example, you see how @ is used as a prefix operator in front of a scalar data structure to return it to its original, listish, state.

Item context is quite important to understand the nature of complex structures, such as arrays, as data containers. Check out this example, where you keep in an array the last value of a progression, and the next to last:

```
my $first = 3;
my @latests;
for ^3 {
    @latests = ($first, $first *= 3 );
}

say @latests;
```

You might expect it to hold something like [27,81], right? There's no way the array values are the same. Well, they are; this expression prints [81 81]. How come?

The problem is that itemization only happens at the end when you are using say. Itemization makes the values become a thing, an item, and thus gels them. You can itemize them by just printing them; however, when you do that, the first and second elements are going to have the same value, since you assign them in the same statement. Let's change it like this:

```
my $first = 3;
my @latests;
for ^3 {
    @latests = (+$first, $first *= 3 );
}
@latests.say
```

By doing this, you're forcing it to be itemized, to become a thing, a value which is the one stored in the array. This will print [27 81], as should be expected.

Extended Identifiers

So far you have seen identifiers that, albeit a bit weird with dashes and apostrophes, are pretty much the same as any other language. However, just in case you have not noticed already, Perl 6 is unlike any other language. Besides regular identifiers (which follow the bare-identifier syntax), it also includes *extended* identifiers. In general, an extended identifier is like a regular identifier followed by what is called an *adverb*. You have already seen what adverbs look like: they are preceded by colons, but, as part of an extended identifier, adverbs will include (or not) behind the colon a regular identifier, followed by a quoting construct. Let's see examples:

```
:won't-do
:will-do<now>
:how're-you«doing»
:<+>
:<©>
```

All of these examples are valid adverbs. Please note how special characters are only admissible *inside* the quotes; that's precisely their function. You can also use any kind of quoting construct, as above. To create an extended identifier, you can combine a regular identifier (which follows the bare identifier syntax) with one or more adverbs:

```
I:<❤>:this
person:age<54>:doing<stuff>
```

Containers using this extended identifier syntax are, of course, perfectly valid as such:

```
say (my $I:<❤>:this = 7)
say (my @person:age<54>:doing<stuff> = [True,False])
```

This syntax will also be used next to define *terms*.

Terms Without Conditions

In a first approximation, terms can be defined as routines that do not need an argument. You already found one in the shape of now, which returns as an Instant the current time. That is the other term defined in the core, time.

```
say time
```

returns the current POSIX time, that is, the number of seconds that have passed since the *epoch*, January 1, 1970.

You can also define these terms for your own purpose. Remember that, since they employ the extended identifier syntax, they can use any character:

```
sub term:<✔> { True }
sub term:<ℜ> { srand(time); return rand }
say "{✔} {ℜ}";
```

In the first case, you are defining a term that is, for all purposes, constant. The advantage here is that you can use any character to define a constant, unlike constants themselves, which are limited to the syntax of regular identifiers. You can also define your own super-random ℜ which seeds the random generator (using srand) using the time term every single time it's called.

Since you are using sigilless variables (a function is also a variable), you need to indicate somehow that they are to be interpreted within a string; this is why you surround them with curly braces. Expressions within a string enclosed with curly braces will be interpreted by Perl 6 and the result placed in the string.

Native Data

An interesting feature of Perl 6 is how it deals with data that uses a native representation in the architecture and operating system the compiler is running; this is what we call *native* data. You are likely to find this type of data when you deal with input/output streams, or when you are going to deal with low-level, native code written in another language (like C). In some other cases, you might simply want to use it for the possible performance improvements.

There are, however, two kind of native types, with or without size. The main difference is that the latter can be used when calling functions created in other languages, through what is called the NativeCall interface, and the former can be used in general. Both will be auto-boxed, that is, converted to a regular (non-native) data type when used within a variable. See Table 7-4.

Table 7-4. *Native types and their autoboxed brethren*

Native type	Autoboxed to	Sized types
int	Int	int8, int16, int32, int64
uint	Int	byte, uint8, uint16, uint32, uint64
num	Num	num32, num64
str	Str	
void		

The importance of sized types will be seen later, when you use the NativeCall interface to work with C programs. The main use of native data is to speed up certain numeric operations:

```
sub bm( &to-time ) { my $start = now; return to-time() ~ "⏰" ~
now - $start; }
my int @natives = ^5_000_000;
```

```
say bm( { [+] @natives } );
my @regular = ^5_000_000;
say bm( { [+] @regular } );
```

In my machine, the whole operation might take up to around 9 seconds, but using native integers will make it three times faster than regular integers.

Finally, I mentioned the void native type above. This native type has no equivalent in Perl 6, but it can be used mainly in interaction with C programming interfaces.

Concluding Remarks

After understanding, in the first chapters, how Perl 6 represents and processes data and simple expressions, this is the first chapter in which, through learning how data (and functions; remember that they are first-class citizens) is stored, you have created your first programs using it.

Perl 6 has a powerful syntax and model for data storage, which includes concepts such as binding and native types. Solving any problem through programming includes, first and foremost, dealing with data representation.

In the next chapters, you will build on this foundation, starting with how functions are defined and processed.

CHAPTER 8

Functions

Defining and Using Functions as First Class Citizens.

Callables: Code, Blocks, and Routines

You have already seen in previous chapters how Perl 6, having functions as first class citizens, can produce chunks of code out of thin air and work with them. The title of this section lists the classes used for functions in increasing order of complexity. All of them are Callable; code is the simplest type that implements that role; blocks can define a *signature* or the name of the variables that will be used inside the code itself; a routine is a block that has its own name and can specify data that is going to be returned via the return statement.

Routines themselves can be of different types; they are most often not used directly. Methods are routines used in classes that keep an implicit reference to the object and its attributes; submethods are special methods within classes that are not inherited. Subs are regular routines defined via the sub keyword. And finally there are macros, which are pieces of code that generate other pieces of code (and which, for the time being, are not fully implemented).

In Perl 6, regular expressions, or regexes, are special methods, being a subclass of Method. You will see the reason for this later on.

© J.J. Merelo 2019
J.J. Merelo, *Perl 6 Quick Syntax Reference*, https://doi.org/10.1007/978-1-4842-4956-7_8

Most of the remaining chapter will be applied to routines in general. You will, in general, use sub, since object-oriented programming is going to be explained in full in a later chapter.

Let's start with the most important part, defining how routines are called and what they return.

Signatures and Captures: Calling Functions and Return Types

Looks simple enough, right? You declare the name you want to give the arguments with which you are going to call the function, and that's that. Maybe you add a type for good measure. Say, for instance, you want to create a deck of cards combining numbers and suits:

```
sub deck( @numbers, @cards ) {
    return @numbers X~ @cards;
}

say deck( 1..3, <bastos espadas>);
say deck( <J Q K>, <♥ ♣ ♠ ♦> );
```

Thus far you have worked with scalar arguments, since that was all that was needed to illustrate the point in the previous chapters. However, here you have a couple of arrays as arguments. What this means is that the arguments are going to be transformed to arrays; in the first case, 1..3 is a Range, but it gets coerced into an array. The sigil that precedes the argument name will be used to check type information. It needs to be that kind of variable, or have a way of being converted into that. Unlike what you saw previously in variable assignments, type checking is a bit stricter, and scalars will not be upgraded to Positionals, or Associative coerced into them. You can, however, do a bit of coercion if you use *slurpy* arguments:

```
sub deck( @cards, *@numbers ) {
    return @numbers X~ @cards;
}
say deck( <bastos espadas>, 1,3,5); # (1bastos 1espadas ..)
say deck( <♥ ♣ ♠ ♦>, "Ace" ); # (Ace♥ Ace♣ Ace♠ Ace♦)
```

Slurpy arguments, preceded by an asterisk, gobble up into an array everything else that's used as an argument. In the first case, every argument is slotted into elements of the array, and in the second case, where a single string is used, it becomes an array with a single element.

You can also restrict the return type for the routine using -->, like so:

```
sub deck( @cards, *@numbers --> Seq ) {
    return @numbers X~ @cards;
}
```

The X operation returns a Sequence; if you try to return anything else, a type check exception will be thrown.

You can also typecheck arguments beyond simply their arrangement, same as when you declare the scope of a variable:

```
sub deck( @cards, UInt $how-many, *@numbers
          --> List ) {
    return (@numbers X~ @cards)[^$how-many];
}
say deck( <bastos espadas>, 4, 1,3,5); # (1bastos 1espadas
3bastos 3espadas)
say deck( <♥ ♣ ♠ ♦>, 2, "Ace" ); # (Ace♥ Ace♣)
```

This code introduces another argument, $how-many, which needs
to be an unsigned integer (Uint). This will restrict the number of cards
produced. At the same time, you are extracting a slice off the Sequence,
which always produces a list, which is why you have changed the
return type.

You already have three arguments, and if you look at the deck call, it
might be difficult to distinguish where an argument finishes and the next
starts. If you've got more than four or five, it's better to name arguments
instead of using their position to know what each argument is. Named
arguments use the pair syntax you saw earlier in this book:

```
sub deck( :@suits, UInt :$how-many = 2, :@cards --> List ) {
    return (@cards X~ @suits)[^$how-many];
}
say deck( suits => <bastos espadas>,
          how-many => 4, cards => (1,3,5) );
my @suits = <♥ ♣ ♠ ♦>;
my @cards = "Ace";
say deck( :@suits, :@cards );
```

Note that you're using a default value for $how-many. Default values
can also be used in Positional arguments, with the same syntax, although
only if they occupy the last positions. The Positional arguments use a
colon, and they indicate at the same time the name of the variable they
are going to use in the routine and the name of the key they will use in the
invocation. In the first call, you use those keys; in the second, however, you
use another form, where the *name* of the variable itself is the key if you use
for calling the same syntax you use for the definition. Besides, you save one
of the named arguments, with the default value kicking in. The output is
the same as before, but maybe a bit of clarity has been achieved.

You might also want the routine to do some transformation for you; you might need the return type or any of the arguments to be a different type. Perl 6 will let you *coerce* arguments and return types on the fly, like so:

```
sub deck( Array(Set) \suits,
          UInt :$how-many = 4, :@cards
          --> Seq(List) ) {

    return (@cards X~
      suits.values.map("❖❖" ~ *.key);)[^$how-many];
}
my $palos = set <bastos espadas>;
say deck( $palos, how-many => 4, cards => (1,3,5) );
```

There are several things you should notice here. First, it illustrates how named and Positional arguments can be used together, as long as Positionals go first. In this case, you declare a Positional argument named \suits.

That's the second thing you should notice. In the context of a routine signature, sigilless variables are useful because they don't force any kind of role on the argument; a sigilless argument can be called, indistinctly, with scalar, Positional, Associative, or even Callable arguments. In this case, however, you use it because, in the third thing you should notice, you are coercing from a set, which is not Positional, to an array, which is. Sigils would change in the process, so you just get rid of them.

You are also returning a Seq, which would be more convenient for iterating, for instance. The class in parentheses is the origin, the one outside is the target in both cases, argument and return type coercion.

Eventually, the set of arguments for a function have a certain level of complexity, and that complexity is captured by the Capture object. A Capture object is a mixture of Positionals and Associatives, and thus can be seen simply as a *mixed* data structure. But it's more than that: it can actually be used to call a function, instead of enumerating the arguments in the routine call. You do that here:

```
sub deck( @suits, UInt $hand = 3, :@cards
          --> Seq(List) ) {

    return (@cards X~  ("❖❖" X~ @suits) )[^$hand];
}
my $capture = \(<Bastos Espadas>,
                :cards("Sota","Caballo","Rey"));
say deck( |$capture );
```

This example, still an evolution of your hand-of-cards generating little program, simplifies the signature, using a default value for the second Positional argument, but the interesting part is where you define a Capture, by inserting a backslash (\) in front of the parentheses. This is a literal definition of the same kind you saw in Chapter 3.

Please note that you're using a $ sigil for this mixture of Positional and Associative.

Even being a Capture, you have to distinguish between calling-this-sub-with-this-variable-which-happens-to-be-a-Capture and using-this-capture-as-the-whole-set-of-arguments-to-this-routine. The vertical bar does precisely that: *capturizes* the variable, turning it into a Capture that will be deconstructed to its set of arguments within the routine itself.

Of course, Perl 6 being a functional language, you can create functions that create other functions:

```
sub dealer( @cards --> Callable ) {
    my  &deck = sub {
        state @cards-we-have = @cards;
        my @shuffled = @cards-we-have.pick: *;
```

```
        my $card = @shuffled.pop;
        @cards-we-have = @shuffled;
        return $card;
    }
    return &deck;
}
```

```
my &deck = dealer( <Bastos Espadas> X~ "❖ ❖" X~ <Sota Caballo
Rey>);
```

```
deck().say for ^3;
# Every time, something like Espadas ❖ ❖ Sota
```

The function `dealer` takes a deck of cards as input and creates another function that deals those cards, storing (via a state variable) the remaining cards. The main issue in this example is that you initialize the state variable `@cards-we-have` with a lexically scoped variable, `@cards`, and return a dealer in the variable `&deck`. These object-like functions are, by themselves, pretty useful and can be used profitably in your programs. You can obviously use it also as an argument, and you can even declare type constraints for it:

```
sub draw( @cards, &drawer:(Positional) ) {
    return drawer(@cards);
}
```

```
my @cards = <Bastos Espadas> X~ "❖ ❖" X~ <Sota Caballo Rey>;
sub first-drawer( @c ) { @c.shift };
sub last-drawer(@c) { @c.pop };
```

```
say draw( @cards, &first-drawer ); # Bastos ❖ ❖ Sota
say draw( @cards, &last-drawer );  # Espadas ❖ ❖ Rey
```

With the & sigil, it's quite clear that the second argument is a function, and it will tell you which card to extract from the deck. You define two of them: one takes the first card, the other the last card. Since the argument declares that the function must take a Positional argument, you just restrict the argument to these functions with the @ sigil, which indicates it's, in effect, a positional argument. You can then call the draw function with these defined ones, remembering to add the sigil at the beginning to indicate you are using the container that contains the function, not calling the function itself.

You are also using pop and shift, two functions that extract the last and first element of an array. Perl 6 includes a whole set of functions for working with arrays, which can also use (since they are superclasses) the List, Any, and Mu functions. You can access them in the complete reference manual at https://docs.perl6.org/type/Array. In general, any Perl 6 class called "A-Class" will host the reference manual at https://docs.perl6.org/type/A-Class.

Subsets and Type Constraints

The type system in Perl 6 takes orientation from object-orientation, but also from functional languages. Subtypes derive types from preexisting ones through conditions, as in "This is like that, except for...." The Perl 6 concept of subsets is one notch down from that, since subsets are not properly types (although they can be used in many occasions that way) but you can leverage them all the same in your programs. You'll use one to restrict the possible numbers a card can use:

```
subset CardNumber of Int where 0 < * <= 10;

sub card( CardNumber $card-number, $suit ) {
    return "$card-number de $suit";
}
say card( 2, "Bastos");
say card( 9, "Espadas");
```

The subset `CardNumber` will restrict cards to numbers 1 to 10. You are using `Whatever` to perform the check; in the same way you did when dealing with expressions, ∗ will represent whatever you want to check for that type. You use a subset instead of a type for the routine signature. It will let through any number that checks out, and fail if it does not, acting exactly like a type check, only it's one you have created on the fly.

Subsets are great and it is good practice to define them for objects that have to do with the problem you're solving. But you can also use them to restrict argument values in the signature itself:

```
sub card( Int $card-number where 0 < * <= 10, $suit ) {
    return "$card-number de $suit";
}
```

This will behave in the same way as before. If your check is relatively complex, it might be better to not burden a routine definition with it, but other than that, it's technically fine to do it that way.

Junctions

I am introducing these objects a bit late in the book, but they are terribly useful when declaring function arguments, so it's about time we talk about them.

Junctions are multiple-valued objects; they can take several values, and they operate with them in parallel, including comparisons:

```
my $cat = "Dead" | "Alive";
say $cat eq "Dead"; # any(True, False)
say $cat eq "Alive"; # any(False, True)
```

Junctions are created using the | particle and can have in principle any number of values. This results in a Junction of type "any," which can be used as stand-ins in all kind of operations, as shown here with equality. The return value, however, will be the effect of having applied that operation to all the components, as is shown by the output.

This is not the only type of Junction available. They are shown in Table 8-1, together to the Boolean value they would collapse to.

Table 8-1. *Types of junctions, their symbols and meaning*

Type	Meaning	Operator
any	True if any of them is True	|
all	True only if all of them are True	&
one	True if only one is True	^
none	True if all of them are True.	N/A

Junctions are of type any by default. If you want to create any other type of Junction, you need to prefix a list with the type:

```
my $cat = one <Dead Alive>;
say "Dead or alive" if $cat eq 'Dead' and $cat eq 'Alive';
```

The expression behind if will be True if and only if just one of the results of the comparison is True. It's True in both cases, so this will print "Dead or alive". As shown in Table 8-1, you can also use

```
my $cat = "Dead" ^ "Alive";
```

Junctions are very useful to constrain the arguments of a routine:

```
sub card( Int $card-number where 0 < * <= 10,
        $suit where "Bastos" | "Espadas" | "Oros" | "Copas" )
{
    return "$card-number de $suit";
}
say card( 2, "Bastos");
say card( 9, "Espadas");
```

This script will write the same as the one above. However, in this case, you are also restricting, via a Junction, the suit you can use to the ones in the Spanish deck. That simple where + Junction statement is equivalent to an equality that would include *, but this is so common that it's shortened to simply the options the argument must follow. If another word was used here, an error like

```
Constraint type check failed in binding to parameter
'$suit'; expected anonymous constraint to be met but got Str
("Diamonds")
```

would be thrown. The fact that it is telling you "it does not meet the anonymous constraint," which might be a bit confusing, would make a best practice to define as a subset any kind of constraint. The solution above, however, is flawless and technically correct.

Smartmatching

You have seen many kinds of equality operators that depend on what they are actually comparing. But sometimes you don't know in advance the actual type of something, for instance, as a function argument. Or you simply don't care. Smartmatch to the rescue. This operator uses the double squiggly lines like this: ~~.

This operator does not care about the types of their operands. It takes a (smart) guess on what you want to compare and tells you if it's true or not. In order to do so, some type coercion might be needed, but smartmatching will do it happily for you. Some of the matching this operator will do for you includes

- Equality comparison independent of the type.

- Does a container belong to a certain class?

- Are two objects equal?

- Is the list pattern the same?

119

- Does the container implement a role?

- Is this element in a Range?

- Is this string a key in a hash?

There are many other uses, and how it acts for a particular class is always intuitive, but sometimes it's more powerful than you would imagine. Of course, it's used also for regular expressions and even checking the state of a file. More on this in later chapters.

Some examples, in order:

```
say "1" ~~ 1;
my $a-set = set <1 2 3>;
say $a-set ~~ Set;
my @bound = <3 33 333>;
my @bind := @bound;
say @bound ~~ @bind;
say @bound ~~ (3, *, 333 );
say @bound ~~ Iterable;
say 3 ~~ ^5;
my %myth-objects =  %(Þor => "Mjólnir",
                      Oðinn => "Hugin") ;
say "Oðinn" ~~ %myth-objects;
```

All of these examples return True. This operator does have a small quirk: it's not symmetric. In most cases you can swap the left- and right-hand side and it will work the same. However, it's actually implemented as a method of the object in the right-hand side, so swapping might work in different ways. For instance,

```
say  (3, *, 333 ) ~~ @bound ;
```

is going to be False, since the object on the left-hand side is no longer an array, and the one on the right is no longer the one that smartmatches against the one on the left.

With Junctions, it will behave as if a comparison would have been followed by a collapse to a single Boolean value, so

```
say "Sota" ~~ "Sota" | "Caballo" | "Rey";
say "As" ~~ "Sota" | "Caballo" | "Rey";
```

will return True and False, and the result of using eq followed by a collapse via so or ?. As a matter of fact, this is what where does in signatures: it smartmatches against the value of the argument.

Decoupling Signatures

You have seen that Perl 6 is able to *capture* all values that are going to be used to invoke a routine in a, well, Capture; in fact, it has also objects, called Signatures, which contain the format of the signature a routine is called with. They are mostly used to check if a routine follows a certain signature via smartmatch.

Sometimes all the possibilities with which a routine is going to be called are not known in advance. You know the general layout, but the details might vary, and several possible types might be used as an argument. There's a straightforward solution: to go sigilless, but then you lose all type information and the possibility of tailoring the implementation to the different types used.

```
my $card-printer = :(Int,Str);
sub print-card( Int $card-number,
                Str $suit,
                &printer where .signature ~~ $card-printer) {
    return printer( $card-number, $suit);
}
```

```
my &de-printer = -> Int $card, Str $suit { "$card de $suit" };
my &printer:<◆> = -> Int $card, Str $suit { "$card ◆ $suit" };
say print-card( 2, "Bastos", &de-printer); # 2 de Bastos
say print-card( 9, "Espadas", &printer:<◆>); # 9 ◆ Espadas
```

The signature is defined in the first line; a literal signature uses a colon preceding a set of parentheses. Within them, you can put anything that you would put in the definition of a routine, up to and including argument names. They are, however, irrelevant: a Signature represents the *structure* of the arguments, not their actual names. This is why here you simply eliminate them to lay the structure bare so that it can be seen more clearly.

The third (positional) argument to the routine is where you use the power of the Signature together with smartmatching. Implicit variables (and objects) behave in the same way in where clauses as in blocks: .signature will be a method applied to the object that will *fill* the argument.

You define two routines; there's nothing extraordinary in them, only that you have used the extended syntax to define the second. It seemed appropriate, since it's that precise symbol it's introducing.

You call the print-card routine twice, once with each defined printer function. They both check out OK since they have the correct signature, so they are called and return the formatted card name.

Multiple Schedule in Functions

Signature checking allows Perl 6 to have another nifty trick: calling different implementations of functions with the same name, depending on how the arguments match the implementation signature. These are called multi, and the technique they follow multiple schedule. At a very basic level, it's like *overloading* a routine with multiple meanings; but, as is usual with Perl 6, it comes with steroids.

```
enum Palo <Bastos Copas Oros Espadas>;
enum Suit <♣ ♦ ♥ ♠>;
multi stringify-card( Palo $p, Int $n ) { "$n de $p" }
multi stringify-card( Suit $s, Int $n ) { "$s\c[EN QUAD]$n" }
say stringify-card( Bastos, 3 );        # 3 de Bastos
say stringify-card( Suit::<♣>, 5 ); # ♣ 5
```

After defining two enums (in the way you learned in Chapter 3), you use those same enums to define two multis, each one dealing with a different kind of names of cards. However, since they are enums, you have to use the fully qualified name, which includes the name of the enum you are using. You save some writing, although you have to use the fully qualified name of suits, since that can't be used directly as an enum. You can save it by using pattern matching for arguments. But, at the same time, it would be interesting to define a prototype all these functions must follow, as a guideline for the Signature you should use if you want to add another. Please also note that multis are, by default, subs. You omit the sub declaration in this case; the declarations above would be equivalent to proto sub.

A proto, or prototype, also creates a link between all the functions that follow it:

```
proto stringify-card( Str, Int) {*}
multi stringify-card( $p where (* ~~ any <Bastos Copas Oros
Espadas>),
                      Int $n ) { "$n de $p" }
multi stringify-card( $s where (* ~~ any <♣ ♦ ♥ ♠>), Int $n )
{ "$s\c[EN QUAD]$n" }
say stringify-card( "Bastos", 3 );
say stringify-card( "♣", 5 );
```

123

You can use this link for processing some information in a cascade:

```
proto stringify-card( | ) {*}
multi stringify-card( Str $p ) { "▸ $p" }
multi stringify-card( $p where
                        (* ~~ any <Bastos Copas Oros Espadas>),
                        Int $n ) {
    samewith "$n de $p"
}
multi stringify-card( $s where (* ~~ any <♣ ♦ ♥ ♠>),
                        Int $n ) {
    samewith "$s\c[EN QUAD]$n"
}
say stringify-card( "Bastos", 3 );    # ▸ 3 de Bastos
say stringify-card( "♣", 5 );         # ▸ ♣ 5
```

This proto for stringify-card relaxes the Signature, leaving a very generic | (which accepts any Signature); you could have also used

```
proto stringify-card( Str, Int $? ) {*}
```

You don't need to insert variable names since they are not actually part of the Signature; however, optional parameters, indicated with a question mark, do need to get at least a sigil. This is why you use a simple sigil followed by a question mark. This declaration would work in the same way as above. It's always advisable to use Signatures as precisely as possible; however, in the case above you don't really know in advance how the cascade processing of cards is going to be used, so let's keep it that way for the time being. A new multi has been introduced and is mainly intended to postprocess the card represented in the strings by prepending the symbol for "Play" in front of any card. Since this is part of the "group," you don't need to use the name of the sub: you use samewith, which calls the *same* multi *with* a new set of arguments, which you provide.

This is only one of the routines that work with a group of multis. The rest of the redispatching functions are shown in Table 8-2.

Table 8-2. *Short description of some redispatching functions*

Command	Meaning
callsame	Calls the next candidate with the *same* arguments, *returning* a result.
callwith	Calls the next candidate with *new* arguments, *returning* a result.
nextsame	Calls the next candidate with the *same* arguments, *doesn't* return a result.
nextwith	Calls the next candidate with *new* arguments, *doesn't* return a result.
nextcallee	Returns what would have been the next function called, and can be assigned to a variable.

Terms and Operators

Sometimes the business logic of your application needs the use of identifiers that escape the constraining realm of alphanumeric characters (in any alphabet). The extended syntax in Perl 6 has been invented exactly for that purpose and allows you to define functions of any arity (that is, number of arguments) that use any kind of characters in the Unicode alphabet. If these functions receive no argument, they are called *terms*. They are called *operators* if they have 1 or more arguments.

For instance, your application logic might tell you to draw a card. Of course, you use a pencil to draw

```
sub term:<✎> {
    return (^10).pick => <♣ ♦ ♥ ♠>.pick
};
say ✎; # 2 => ♥, for instance.
```

You have defined the term ✏ to draw cards, and it will draw a different one every time. Once it's defined, you don't need parentheses (since it needs no argument) or the word term itself; you just use it directly. You use the method `pick`, which gets a random element every time out of an infinite deck.

How to do the same with a finite deck is left to the interested reader. Hint: Use state variables to keep cards that have already been drawn.

Since cards are naturally a couple consisting of a suit and a number, you use a pair to hold them. But is there an easy way to create them? Once again, your business logic might lead you to define an operator for an easier (or more straightforward) definition. For instance, you can use them to define and build playing cards:

```
sub infix:<♢>   (Str $s, Int $n) { $s => $n };
sub postfix:<♣> (Int $n ) { "♣" ♢ $n };
sub postfix:<♦> (Int $n ) { "♦" ♢ $n };
sub postfix:<♥> (Int $n ) { "♥" ♢ $n };
sub postfix:<♠> (Int $n ) { "♠" ♢ $n };
say qq:to/CARDS/;
{10♦}
{6♥}
{2♠}
{4♣}
CARDS
```

You are defining two kinds of operators here: infix (with two arguments and used in the middle) and postfix (single argument, goes behind the argument). Table 8-3 shows all the types of operators you can define and their meanings.

Table 8-3. *Descriptors of the positions of operators and their characteristics*

Operator type	Arity	Meaning
Postfix	1	Goes behind its argument
Prefix	1	Goes in front of its argument
Infix	2	Goes in the middle of its arguments
Circumfix	1	Goes around its argument
Postcircumfix	2	First argument goes before, second is surrounded by operator

In this case, the character representing the suits is defined as a postfix operator, while the gear building the card is an infix operator.

Since printing pairs might include arrows and you don't want them in this case, you are using another construct to print. First, surrounding any expression with {} in a string will evaluate that string. Then, you are using a quoting construct, qq:to/WORD/, which allows you to define multiline strings. The double-q indicates that it's not literal (that would be the single q), but that evaluation is performed on it. This would print an aligned set of cards, this way:

```
♦    10
♥    6
♠    2
♣    4
```

It's interesting to note that Perl 6 is a very coherent language, with most of its interpreter written using Perl 6 itself. This gives you many examples of the use of these operators in the language itself. The {} that extracts the value attached to a hash's key, for instance, is defined as a postcircumfix operator that takes as arguments the hash and the key. The square brackets themselves are a circumfix operator that builds arrays. The letter I that defines the imaginary part of a complex number is also defined that way.

Concluding Remarks

This chapter has been devoted to functions. You have seen how to define them, including the very special terms and operators, which are nothing but functions with funny names (and characters). Captures and signatures are two faces of the same thing: captures abstract the arguments a routine is called with; signatures abstract the types of the arguments and how they are organized.

Constraints of types in signatures, also called contracts in other languages, have led you to two interesting concepts: Junctions, or ways to express alternative states or values in the same way, and smartmatch, an operator that is used for multi-type matching.

Multiple schedule in functions makes Perl 6, yet again, closer to functional languages, where a similar concept called *pattern matching* is the default way of defining functions.

All in all, these features make Perl 6 a language that is able to make the program you write as close as possible to your business logic, making it reflect visually the actual objects you will be working with. Being so expressive, programs tend to be shorter and this length (and expressiveness) also makes parsing the language more efficient.

However, Perl 6 is also a multiparadigm language. You will see how classes are defined in the next chapter.

CHAPTER 9

Roles and Classes

Bundling Code and Data in the Same Block and Reusing It Is the Main Part Roles and Classes Play in So-Called Object-Oriented Languages

Object-oriented programming has been one of the prevailing paradigms in computing in the last few decades. It provides easy abstractions of the problem domain and a way to model it that *feels* natural. However, there are many ways to orient your programming to objects. As is usual in Perl 6, it does not opt for one of them: it includes them all and lets the user pick their preferred one. This style of programming does not preclude the other styles you have seen: you can do functional-style programming with objects or object-oriented style accessing functions via their class interface.

In this chapter, you will program objects and classes, but you'll also explore roles and more precise and exotic ways to deal with objects.

Creating Classes and Objects

Classes describe data structures and functions that operate on them directly. They *instantiate* to objects, that is, an object is an *example* or *instance* of a class. Objects in a class can be declared and used as such.

© J.J. Merelo 2019
J.J. Merelo, *Perl 6 Quick Syntax Reference*, https://doi.org/10.1007/978-1-4842-4956-7_9

"Class" and "type" can be used interchangeably in this context; in Perl 6, all types are classes since they can be instantiated and have methods attached to them.

You have already seen many built-in types; all types in Perl 6 are actually classes. In most built-in types, creation is done implicitly by using literals or by any operation that works on them. But objects are created via the method new; you can use it if you want:

```
say (my $new-int = Int.new(3)) ; # 3
```

When I say that everything is an object, I also mean classes themselves. They are, as a matter of fact, called *type objects* and you can use them as you would any other object:

```
my $Simply-an-Int = Int;
say (my $new-int = $Simply-an-Int.new(3)); #3
```

$Simply-an-Int is a type object, which is the same as a class and can use new as the rest of the classes can. There should be some way to distinguish between simply-objects and type-objects, right? As a matter of fact, there is a mechanism called a *type smiley* that can be used in signatures to distinguish between them.

```
proto stringify-card( Str, |) {*}
multi stringify-card( $s where (* ~~ any <♣ ♦ ♥ ♠>), Any:D $n )
{ "$s\c[EN QUAD]$n" }
multi stringify-card( $s where (* ~~ any <♣ ♦ ♥ ♠>), Any:U $n )
{
    "$s\c[EN QUAD]" ~ (1..10).pick;
}
say stringify-card( "♣", 5 );
say stringify-card( "♥", Int );
```

Type smileys add a :D or :U (as in "Definite" or "Un-definite") to indicate an object instance or a type object. In the second multi, you use a type object simply to indicate that you should generate the card value randomly; but $n does contain the type and it could be used in any way you want, for instance generating an element of that type from the type object.

```
"$s\c[EN QUAD]" ~ $n.new((1..10).pick);
```

The output would be exactly the same in this case, only you have ensured that you generated an object of that specific type. Please note also that you have relaxed the type in the signature to Any. All built-in types subclass Any (except Junctions, as a matter of fact). Since the argument value will smartmatch the definition, most types, including Int, will meet that constraint, that is, they will be type objects (denoted by the :U type smiley) that subclass Any (the type of the argument).

This isn't the only way to deal with types in Signatures; Perl 6 offers *type captures* that take the value of the type of a particular variable:

```
sub stringify-card( $s, ::T $n ) {
    when T ~~ Str { "$n of $s" }
    when T ~~ Int { "$n\c[EN QUAD]$s" }
    default { "$n$s" }
}
say stringify-card( "♣", 5 );      # 5 ♣
say stringify-card( "♥", "Ace" ); # Ace of ♥
```

Type captures are expressed with two colons and the name of the container where you want the class kept. You use a when clause and smartmatch to distinguish between the different types $n will use, depending on whether it's a number or a symbol.

Think of these double colons as a sigil, just like @ or $, that tells you that the identifier is going to hold a type.

You can use the additional syntax above in any kind of routine, but you will focus on the routines that act on object instances, which are called *methods*. The main difference with respect to regular routines is they have as an implicit argument the object itself. You have already seen that they are called with a period that acts as a postfix to the object name. For instance, you use .match to match part of a string:

```
"J ♣".match("J").say  # ⌈J⌋
```

Introspection

You have already seen methods with ^ prefixed, as in ^name. These are invocations of methods in the meta-object protocol, acting on the class that generates all classes. As the objects are instances of classes, type objects are instances of meta-classes. And Perl 6 allows you to access the inner working of every one of these levels. You can find this higher-order object by using the HOW method:

```
"J ♣".HOW.say; #  Perl6::Metamodel::ClassHOW.new
```

HOW is not a proposition, but an acronym for Higher Order Working. As a matter of fact, all ^ prefixed methods are methods of these objects, so the code above is equivalent to

```
"J ♣".HOW.name("").say
```

Delving into the inner working of the classes is called introspection. You saw this in Chapter 7, along with ^methods and ^mro. But there are other (meta) methods you can use; see Table 9-1.

Table 9-1. *Some meta methods*

Metamethod	What it does
can($name)	Returns the list of methods that use that name
lookup($name)	Returns the first method with that name, or an undefined value if it does not exist
attributes()	Returns the list of instance variables

You don't need to access these metamethods to check whether you can do something with an object or not. Preceding a method name with ? will call the method if it exists or will return Nil if it does not.

```
for (3, 1..3, "m" ) -> $m {
    .say with $m.?bounds()
}
```

This calls .bounds, which is a method that is used exclusively by Ranges, on several objects. Since with statements are only run if the result is defined, it will only print something in the second element of the list, which is effectively a Range.

Declaring and Using a Class

You can also create your own classes:

```
class Card {
    has $.value;
    has $.suit;
    method show() { "$!value of $!suit" }
}
my Card $deuce = Card.new( value => 2, suit => '♥' );
say $deuce.perl;
say $deuce.show;
```

A class is declared with the class keyword. The class code is enclosed in brackets, and it includes methods and attributes. Methods are declared with the keyword has, and they are instance variables that will receive a value when a new object of that class is created.

These attributes use twigils: the usual sigil representing the role, followed by a period in this case, indicating that they are public attributes. This means that the .value (and .suit) methods are automatically generated. You can use them, for instance, here:

```
say $deuce.map( { .value, .suit } ); # ((2 ♥))
```

map aliases $deuce to the default variable, $_, and .value and .suit act on them.

You can declare a single method, show, which returns a string with the value. Within this method, the values of the instance variables are present. You can use the method form ($.value) to access them, but instead you will use a new sigil, $!, which is short for self.; $!attribute retrieves the value of the attribute *attribute* for the current object. That's the meaning of $!value and $!suit in the example above.

You can also use self, which is a term that represents the object within its methods; the same effect can be achieved with

```
method show() { "{self.value} of $!suit" }
```

In this case, since self is not preceded by a sigil, you need the curly braces to evaluate it inside a string.

Since all classes are instances of Mu, there are some methods that they all have. .perl is one of them: it yields a *machine-readable* representation of the object, which could theoretically be used to instantiate it if evaluated.

The example above uses the default new to create an object; this default new has a signature that includes all instance variables as named arguments. But you can, of course, add to that default another one:

```
class Card {
    has $!value;
    has $!suit;
    multi method new ($value, $suit ) {
        return self.bless( :$value, :$suit );
    }
    submethod BUILD( :$!value, :$!suit ) {}
    method show() { "$!value of $!suit" }
}
my Card $deuce = Card.new( 2, '♥' );
say $deuce.perl; # Card.new
say $deuce.show; # 2 of ♥
```

This is especially necessary if you use hidden attributes, as above. Hidden attributes use the ! twigil to indicate both the fact that they are going to be hidden (from .perl also) and that there's going to be no accessor created for them. You can still use the default new to add values, but there's not much point in hiding the implementation if you are going to expose it in the documentation that indicates how to instantiate an object.

The new new needs to be declared as a multi if you don't want to override the default new (which might be used anyway by subclasses); within it, you call self.bless with the signature of the default constructor; as you know, :$value is equivalent to value => $value. But what bless does is to start the building phase of the object. Since you are not using the default constructor, you need to specify it too.

Building an object takes place in different phases, in the order shown in Table 9-2.

Table 9-2. *Essential phasers*

Phase	Action
BUILD	Assigns values to instance variables when creating an object
TWEAK	Assigns values to instance variables after the object has been created

In a class you will use submethods to implement these *phasers*. They will always be called implicitly from the default new or (almost) explicitly by using bless, in this order:

new or bless → BUILD → TWEAK

Actually, there's no code in the definition of the submethod. By using the attributes in the signature, the values BUILD is called with will be bound directly to them, without needing to assign them explicitly in the body of the submethod.

There's an alternative to this, if you haven't overridden the default constructor: you can call it explicitly via

```
return Card.new( :$value, :$suit );
```

as you would use from outside the class. This will get exactly the same result.

But you are still using show to get the value; your classes can overload the methods that every class has (mentioned in Chapter 6), such as .perl. But to show the object you will overload .gist by simply changing the name of that method to gist:

```
method gist() { "$!value of $!suit" }
```

And then you can use directly

```
say $deuce
```

which will call that method.

You can also assign default values to instance variables. Here you use a new attribute, $!victories, to store the number of times a particular card has won:

```
class Card {
    has $.value;
    has $.suit;
    has $!victories = 0;
    method new ($value, $suit ) {
        return self.bless( :$value, :$suit );
    }
    submethod BUILD( :$!value, :$!suit ) {}
    method better-than( Card $c ) {
      if $c.suit eq $!suit {
          if $!value > $c.value {
              $!victories++;
              return True
          } else {
              return False;
          }
      } else {
          return False;
      }
    }
    method gist() { "$!value of $!suit  won $!victories times" }
}
my Card $deuce = Card.new( 2, '♥' );
say $deuce;  # Will print "2 of ♥  won 0 times"
say Card.new( 3, '♥' ).better-than( $deuce );
say $deuce.better-than: Card.new( 3, '♦' );
say $deuce.better-than: Card.new( 1, '♥' );
say $deuce; # Will print "2 of ♥  won 1 times"
```

In general, class attributes follow a syntax that is close to scope declaration or signatures; default values are assigned by appending the equal sign and the value you want.

Please observe that, despite using different twigils for declaration, you always use the ! twigil to retrieve their value. Here you are also using the colon-based way of invoking methods, which you have seen before when using map and other objects. It's simply a cleaner and simple alternative to using parentheses, but you can use it only if it's the last invocation in a chain.

The new method that you have introduced takes only another Card, and it returns True if the value is higher and they belong to the same suit. If it does not belong to the same suit, you can't say if it's better or worse (it will depend on the game), so you return False.

Since methods are actually routines, they can also be multiple scheduled:

```
class Card {
    has $.value;
    has $.suit;
    method new ($value, $suit ) {
      return self.bless( :$value, :$suit );
    }
    submethod BUILD( :$!value, :$!suit ) {}
    multi method better-than( Card $s where $s.suit eq "Joker":
    Card $c) {
      return True
    }

    multi method better-than( Card $s: Card $c where *.suit eq
    $!suit) {
      if $s.value > $c.value {
          return True
      } else {
```

```
        return False;
    }
  }
  multi method better-than( Card $s: Card $c where *.suit ne
  $!suit) {
    return False;
  }

}
my Card $deuce = Card.new( 2, '♥' );
say Card.new( 3, '♥' ).better-than( $deuce );
say $deuce.better-than: Card.new( 3, '♦' );
say Card.new( 0, "Joker" ).better-than( $deuce );
```

You previously had a rather long double test that would need to be tested rather extensively with all possible values considered. However, multiple schedule allows you to use the signature of the method itself to decide which path to take and an argument constraint can be used to define that. This is what you do in this new version of the code. But you do something more: use a colon as part of the signature. In a first approximation, a colon is a separator that allows you to identify the invoker (to the left) and the rest of the Signature (to the right). From that point of view, it's simply an alias: instead of using self or the straightforward access to attributes using $!, you use the name of the variable (and its public accessors) to do the same.

But this part of the Signature also has the same advantages as the rest: you can constrain it, so that you can direct a method to a implementation by just putting constraints on the attributes of an object. The first multi does that: let's say a Joker beats every other card. You will be using "Joker" as a suit, with value equal to 0, so if the suit of a card is a Joker, well, it's going to always return True. This method will only be called in objects whose suit is a Joker.

This might all seem like syntactic sugar for saving ifs and elses. But ifs can be unwieldy if there are many cases, and the interpreter will be able to work with these methods definitions much more efficiently. It can cache the result of these method calls much more efficiently, for instance. This is also a more functional way of programming, matching patterns rather than executing multiple decisions.

Creating Roles: Methods and Attributes

There are many ways to understand object orientation beyond the basic definition that uses encapsulation, code reuse, and (maybe) inheritance. One of the first divisions stems when you talk about creating new classes out of old ones. You can *compose* classes to create new ones, you can *implement* the interface but not include the code, or you can simply reuse the code by including attributes that are objects of those classes. That is, you can reuse code, reuse interfaces, or both. And once code is going to be reused, you can throw in instance variables or not. On top of that, and somewhat orthogonally, you can also decide whether to make classes generic (that is, applied to any other class) or specific, so that the objects they can be applied to are baked in.

As in many other aspects, Perl 6 does not make any kind of choice for you. It allows you to reuse code, interfaces, instance variables, and just about anything. Or not. You decide how to actually write your code and enforce its conventions. In Perl 6, roles are the way to compose and reuse code, interfaces, or both.

Roles are data structures that include attributes and methods and can also be generic. A class *does* (implement or compose) a role, including all the code and attributes of that role as part of itself. Roles are thus *composed* or *mixed-in* or, if they include non-implemented methods, *implemented* by a particular class.

Here you will use the word role to define them:

```
role Card-values {
    has @.values;
    method one { @!values.pick };
}

class Card-types does Card-values {
    has @.suits;
    method get-one { [@!suits.pick, self.one ] };
}

my @values = (2..10);
@values = @values.append( <J Q K Ace> );
my $french-cards = Card-types.new( :@values, suits => <♦ ♠ ♥
♣> );
say $french-cards.get-one;
```

You have defined a role that stores card values, which can be tricky and not reduced to simple numbers in a Range. You *compose* that role using does into a class that includes suits. Since Card-values is composed into Card-types, Card-types includes all attributes and methods that Card-values declares. The new attribute that Card-types declares is on the same standing as the one mixed in, and the default constructors uses both; you use self.one to invoke the method, since the method one is already part of the type.

This kind of object building makes sense. On one hand, Card-types is not a Card-value, so direct inheritance would not make sense. On the other hand, declaring a Card-values attribute would not make the values intrinsic, or a part, of the object, so you would still need to call it explicitly using the attribute as an object.

In fact, it would make more sense to have suits also as a role:

```
role Card-values {
    has @.values;
    method one-value { @!values.pick };
}
role Card-suits {
    has @.suits;
    method one-suit { @!suits.pick };
}
class Card-types does Card-values does Card-suits {
    method get-one { [self.one-value, self.one-suit ] };
}
```

This will work the same as before. Card-types is mixing in two roles and using their interface to generate a random card. Simply adding as many does clauses as you want will mix the roles you need in your class.

But of course there are many kind of suits and card values. And roles have a very interesting feature: they can be parametrized, that is, they can be defined generically with one or several types left for the developer to pick:

```
role Card-values[::T] {
    has Str $.name;
    method one { T.pick };
    method better-than ( T \lhs, T \rhs ) {
        return lhs < rhs;
    };
}
enum french-digits <② ③ ④ J Q K Ace>;
enum spanish-digits <2. 3. 4. Sota Caballo Rey As>;
class French-card-values does Card-values[french-digits] { };
class Spanish-card-values does Card-values[spanish-digits] { };
my $french-cards = French-card-values.new( name => "French" );
```

```
say $french-cards.better-than( french-digits::«③», french-
digits::«J»);
my $spanish-cards = Spanish-card-values.new( name => "Española" );
say $spanish-cards.better-than( Rey, Sota );
```

The parametrization goes in square brackets, right after the name of the role you want parametrized. It uses in this case a type capture, as you saw previously in this chapter, but it can also use a variable. The nice thing about type captures is that the type can later be used to define instance variables or method calls, as in this case.

When instantiating a role by using a type on it, you must make sure that it can do whatever it's supposed to do inside the role. There are two things it does here: use the method .pick, which is actually present in Any and thus in any of its subclasses (remember, all the core classes except for Junction), and use numeric comparison via <. This is actually where you are leveraging the implicit order in enums: they are ranked in the same order they are declared. Since you don't know in advance the type, it's safer to use sigilless variables to hold their values; these variables will be able to keep it even if it's Associative or Positional.

When using the enums, you will need to type the fully qualified name, with the enum name and the symbol shown here: french-digits::«③». It's not going to be needed in the case it's a regular string (like J) but you can use it anyway for clarity.

The defined classes, as a matter of fact, do not have any code of their own and are more a renaming of the parametrized role. In these cases, you can use a feature called *role punning*, which consists of using directly (possibly parametrized) roles as if they were classes:

```
my $french-cards = Card-values[french-digits].new( name =>
"French" );
my $spanish-cards = Card-values[spanish-digits].new( name =>
"Española" );
```

Eliminating the class definition in the example here and substituting those lines will give you exactly the same result. Although Card-values[french-digits] is a (parametrized) role, not a class, by punning you can create instances of it.

Giving, Using, and Mixing in Roles

The Perl 6 system is quite flexible regarding how containers behave at runtime. A remarkable thing it can do is to mix in roles into a value using but:

```
role Card {
    method Str(::T:) {
        when T ~~ Str {
            my @pair = self.comb;
            return @pair[0] ~ " of " ~ @pair[1..*].join("");
        }
        when T ~~ Pair {
            return self.value ~ " of " ~ self.key;
        }
    }
}
my $deuce = "2♠" but Card;
say $deuce.Str; # 2 of ♠
my $ace = :Bastos("As") but Card;
say $ace.Str;   # As of Bastos
```

The but infix operator mixes the value to its left with the role, object, or class to its right. In this case, it's a simple scalar, but by mixing in the "Card" role you have managed to give it a nice interface that converts it to a string in a more or less uniform way independently of it being defined as a Str or as a Pair. In this case, the profusion of colons in the definition of the Str method use a type capture to capture the type of the object; since it's followed by a colon it means that it's going to be applied to the object itself, to self. This kind of flexibility, as well as the fact that you can apply it directly to an object, is very unique and allows you to work with values, adding functionality to them without needing to define new types. The type of that last value in $ace will be Pair+{Card}, indicating that it's a Pair object, but with Card mixed in.

If a simple object, such as a scalar, is mixed in, an anonymous role will be created. This will transparent, however, although calling methods of the mixed-in object will access that "part" of it:

```
my $deuce = "2♠" but 2;
my $ace   = "Ace ♠" but 100;
say $deuce.^name;              # Str+{<anon|1>}
say $deuce.Int < $ace.Int;   # True
```

You can also associate roles to containers by using the same keyword that is used to define classes, does:

```
role Hand {
    method draw () { self.pick };
}
my @my-hand does Hand = <5♠ 3♦ 8♦>;
say @my-hand.pick;
```

@my-hand is a simple array, but you mix in the Hand role, allowing it to use the draw method, as shown here.

Please note that does cannot be used, due to a bug, on scalar variables.

Inheritance

Inheritance, together with encapsulation, are two of the mainstays of object-oriented programming. Inheritance expresses the relationship is-a between two classes; a particular type of card game is-a (more generic) card game or simply a game. Therefore, Perl 6 uses is to express inheritance or subclassing:

```
class Game {
    has Str $.name;
    method score( @deck ) { ... };
}
class Brisca is Game {
    has %!scores = { As => 11,
                     3 => 10,
                     Rey => 4,
                     Caballo => 3,
                     Sota => 2 };

    method score( @deck ) {
        my $score = 0;
        for @deck.grep( any %!scores.keys) -> $c {
            $score += %!scores{$c};
        }
        return $score;
    }
}
class Guiñote is Game {
    has Int $.diez-de-últimas;
    has %!scores = { As => 11,
                     3 => 10,
                     Rey => 4,
```

```
                    Caballo => 2,
                    Sota => 3 };

    method score( @deck ) {
        my $score = $!diez-de-últimas;
        for @deck.grep( any %!scores.keys )   -> $c {
            $score += %!scores{$c};
        }
        return $score;
    }
}
my @deck = <As 3 7 8 Rey Caballo>;
my Brisca $game1 .= new: name => 'brisca1' ;
my $game2 = Guiñote.new( name => 'Este guiñote', diez-de-
últimas => 10 );

say $game1.score( @deck ); # 28
say $game2.score( @deck ); # 37
```

You define a base class, Game. Card games in Spain are similar to modern card games: you draw a hand, and choose a card from your hand, which you play. If the score of that card is better than the other, you win both cards; if not, the other wins. When the game finishes, you have a pile of cards and you get a score, depending on the inherent score in the cards and other things like the fact that you won the last draw (*diez de últimas*, ten from the last one). There are different games (and they are played differently in different regions and in Latin America) but the baseline is that the pile of cards is scored in a different way, according to card values and additional victories you might have won during the game. But everyone has a deck-based score, which is why you define a score method. By using the yadda yadda yadda operator (...) you make this base class uninstantiable and force all subclasses to reimplement it; Game will be thus an abstract base class, with no real code.

This operator can be used in roles, too, forcing those classes mixing the role to reimplement it.

Besides this method, the subclasses will also inherit the instance variable $!name. Only public instance variables will be inherited; private (those declared with the ! twigil) will remain hidden, or private, also to derived classes. If you need to use them, you will have to define a public interface to these private variables, considering that you will not be able to initialize them from the constructor, only in the TWEAK phase through the public interface.

Methods can also be private. Let's redefine the Guiñote class in the following way:

```
class Guiñote is Game {
    has Int $.diez-de-últimas;

    method !_score-card( $c ) {
        my %scores = :11As,
        3 => 10, :4Rey, :2Caballo, :3Sota;
        return %scores{$c} if $c ~~ any %scores.keys
    }

    method score( @deck ) {
        my $score = $!diez-de-últimas;
        $score += self!_score-card($_) for @deck;
        return $score;
    }
}
```

Private methods are flagged with the ! sigil, and they use self!method-name to be invoked. The period gives access to *public* methods, while ! is, in this class realm, an indicator of private or hidden activities, such as attributes or methods. Conventionally you are going to be using a preceding underscore (_) as a visual indicator of this hiddenness. Hidden methods are obviously not inherited and, in fact, are hidden to anything but the class itself.

The two derived classes use different scoring tables, with the main difference being in the way how you score the Sota (Jack) and Caballo (Horseman, equivalent to Queen in other decks) but also the fact that Guiñote uses "diez de últimas" to add to final score before counting the deck score. The classes need to implement the score or creating an object out of them will fail. The two classes use grep and a Junction to filter out any card whose score is 0. any %!scores.keys creates an any Junction, and grep will match only those cards that correspond to any of the keys.

You use a different syntax for instantiation and definition. You declare the class of the first game, which allows you to use .= to call the new method and create an instance. In general, a op= b is equivalent to a = a op b. Perl 6 generalizes that with method calls: a-class a .= new is equivalent to a = a-class.new. This is the syntax you're using here. You don't need to declare the class in the second case: duck-typing in Perl 6 will automatically assign the class Guiñote to the created object.

Inherited classes can have as static type the base class:

```
my @deck = <As 3 7 8 Rey Sota>;
```

```
my Game $game1 = Brisca.new: name => 'brisca1' ;
my Game $game2 = Guiñote.new( name => 'Este guiñote', :Odiez-
de-últimas );
say $game1.score( @deck );
say $game2.score( @deck );
```

Declaring a variable as the base class will prevent it from being instantiated in a class not in the hierarchy. However, you will be able to assign as a value a different subclass:

```
my Game $game = Brisca.new: name => 'brisca1';
say $game.score( @deck );
$game = Guiñote.new( name => 'Este guiñote', :0diez-de-últimas );
say $game.score( @deck );
```

You are reusing the same variable, which is able to accommodate a dynamic type that is anywhere in the hierarchy.

Concluding Remarks

Object orientation in Perl 6 has two key concepts: roles and classes. Roles are mixed in classes, but also in objects and variables, and classes are inherited, with subclasses taking instance variables and methods from the base class. Additionally, you now know to deal with class objects in signatures, and you should now understand the meta-object protocol a bit better.

You should be able to design and work with a class hierarchy, including roles, by now. In the next chapter, you will integrate this knowledge in higher-level structures, modules, that will be used to create multi-file, complex programs.

CHAPTER 10

Modules

Grouping Functionality in Files for Reuse and Abstraction

A module packages a host of functionalities into a single file, often under a single name. Being as it is a multi-paradigm language, these modules come under different flavors, but two rough categories: solo routines and classes/roles/grammars. As you have seen previously, Perl 6 packs most functionality into classes, but not all of them are, and of course, it's up to you to decide which one is the best for your problem.

Modularity helps keep code files simple and coherent; it also helps document and distribute work among them. Let's start with the creation of modules.

Reusing Code

Perl 6 introduces the concept of a *compunit*, or *compilation unit*, which is code that is analyzed and compiled at the same time. The scripts you have seen so far, being contained in a single file, are compunits; when you split your code in different files, one of them the *main* file and the rest, including libraries that are loaded when the file is run, every one of them is a compunit.

In general, you should try to create loadable compunits, which are basically libraries, that will be functionally coherent; they are called *packages.* Packages really create nothing more than a namespace, which will help to avoid clashes with other names; in practice, they are little

© J.J. Merelo 2019
J.J. Merelo, *Perl 6 Quick Syntax Reference*, https://doi.org/10.1007/978-1-4842-4956-7_10

more than a generic name for *modules, classes,* and *grammars* (which are actually a type of classes). They can be used directly to, well, package code and identifiers within a namespace:

```
package Pack {
    our $packed = 7; say $packed
}
```

Packages include code that has some functional relationship into a single file, although this is more a convention than a syntax requirement. Perl 6 uses the *module* denomination as a generic for all kind of reusable code under a single namespace; this and other types of packages create separate namespaces so that you can reuse identifiers in any number of them and they don't clash with each other.

```
module Draw-Two {

    our sub draw-two( --> Slip ) {
        state @deck = 1..10 X <♠ ♦ ♣ ♥>;
        if @deck {
            my @shuffle = @deck.pick: *;
            my Slip $draw = (@shuffle.pop, @shuffle.pop).Slip;
            @deck = @shuffle;
            return $draw;
        } else {
            return [].Slip;
        }

    }
}

say gather {
    while my $new-draw = Draw-Two::draw-two() {
        given $new-draw {
            .say;
```

```
        take $_;
      }
    }
}
```

Here, you define a module called Draw-Two, with a single sub called draw-too. It's not a very common name, but you never know and anyway a module also defines a scope within which data can be shared. This subroutine will return a Slip, which is basically an embeddable list: push a Slip to a list, and it will *slip* into the list, inserting the elements of the Slip as consecutive elements in the list, instead of creating a nested list. This is useful in your little program, where you will return a shuffled deck of cards.

You can see another interesting container declaration feature here: your is used, instead of my (which you saw in Chapter 7). By default, subs get lexical scope, so you need to say this explicitly. Subs and any other container declared this way have package scope but, unlike lexical scope variables (declared with my), you will be able to use them outside the module as long as you employ the fully qualified name (which includes the package name). Since by default routines have lexical scope, this is a feature you will be using often to create functionality that can be accessed from *outside* where they were originally declared. You can, of course, use it for variables too:

```
package Pack {
    our $packed = 7;
};
say $Pack::packed
```

Please note that the sigil $ moves to the front when you use the FQN, or fully qualified name, of the variable.

The routine uses a state variable (see Chapter 7) to draw cards in couples, returning them as a two-element (cards) list of two elements (number and suit). It will return an empty Slip when the deck is exhausted.

The module functionality is readily available when declared. Since you want to gather all elements, drawn in twos in a shuffled deck, which will be a new list, you use gather/take. The gather statement precedes loops or other statements, slurping in a list of all data structures that are issued to the take command. In this case, using given, you also print what has been drawn before *slipping* it the deck. This gather/take loop will print the whole deck twice: once in couples (the say inside given) and once the whole list (the say right before gather).

Packages are a path to modularity. The best practice is to give each module its own file, which conventionally use the .pm6 extension (as in Perl Module 6). Inside a file like this, you can use the unit declaration at the beginning of the file to indicate all that follows is part of the same namespace, thus saving indentation and braces:

```
unit module Draw-Two;
our sub draw-two( --> Slip ) {
    state @deck = 1..10 X~ <♠ ♦ ♣ ♥>;
    if @deck {
        my @shuffle = @deck.pick: *;
        my Slip $draw = (@shuffle.pop, @shuffle.pop).Slip;
        @deck = @shuffle;
        return $draw;
    } else {
        return [].Slip;
    }

}
```

This will go to a file that customarily takes the same name as the module, with the extension .pm6, that is, Draw-Two.pm6. You usually use kebab case (with the dash separating words) and caps everywhere to give names to modules and classes, which are both packages; there's actually no conventional distinction between them.

As a matter of fact, you can use the `unit` keyword on classes too:

```
unit class Card-Values;

has @.values;
method one { @!values.pick };
method better-than ( $lhs, $rhs ) {
    return @!values.first( * eq $lhs, :kv )[0] > @!values.
first( * eq $rhs, :kv )[0];
};
```

The effect is exactly the same: the rest of the file is understood as the declaration of the class `Card-Values`, and you don't need to use curly braces to surround them.

Classes and modules defined this way need to be imported in the main program for you to use them. But first you need to learn about traits and how they are used extensively in packages.

Traits or Container Properties

Traits are container properties that are enforced at compile time; additionally to the properties that are implied in the container itself, such as the type or its dynamic type, additional properties can be enforced via *traits*, which are orthogonal to the type. Since they act at compile time, they are not aware of the content and can actually be used to shape it, constrain its representation, or create code that will be run at object creation, for instance.

Traits can be applied to every kind of container. In general, they go *after* the container they modify, use the keyword `if`, and are followed by the name of the trait and, in some cases, parameters.

You have already seen `is` used for declaring the superclass of a class. This usage is coherent with using it to declare traits, since both refer to representation or shape of the variable itself.

A list of the most important traits is found in Table 10-1.

Table 10-1. *Most frequent traits*

Trait	Applies to	Meaning
copy	Parameters	The variable will be a copy of the original and can thus be modified.
rw	Parameters, attributes, routines	It can be written to and keep the value in the case of a parameter. It generates a write accessor for an attribute. In the case of a routine, it indicates that its return value can be assigned to.
readonly	Parameters, attributes	Can only be read; this is the default in the case of attributes and parameters, and is generally not used.
tighter, equiv, looser	Operators	Precedence rules. Its argument is the operator with whose precedence can be compared.
assoc	Operators	Associativity, that is, how the occurrence of several operators in a row is interpreted: left, right, chain, list. If a value of "non" is used, using the operator in an associative way will raise an error.
default	Attributes, variables, routines	Default value when it's nullified by having Nil assigned. Needs an argument with the value. In the case of routines, it will be called by default if no signature matches.
required	Attributes	Needs to be assigned a value when an object is created.
DEPRECATED	Attributes	Indicates it's probably not going to be present in the next versions.
export	Routines, classes	Flags a routine in a module as exportable, with the name to be used as argument.
pure	Routines	Flags a routine as being a first-class function with no secondary effects.

This example will build on the classes you have already seen to add a number of traits:

```
class Card-Values {
    has @.values is rw  is required;
    has $.pintan is rw is default("Bastos") = "Espadas";
    method one() is DEPRECATED { @!values.pick ~ $!pintan } ;
    method draw( $cards = 1 ) { (@!values.pick: $cards ) X~
$!pintan };
}

my Card-Values $cards .= new: values => <As Sota Caballo Rey>;
# Will print a message complaining about deprecated code
say $cards.one;
$cards.pintan = Nil;
say $cards.draw;
$cards.values =  ("Ace", 2..10, <J Q K>).flat;
say $cards.draw( 2 );
```

This code defines two attributes with read and write access, which creates an object.attribute accessor that can be modified; you use it to change the values of the cards as well as the suit. The values of the cards will be required, so object creation will fail if those values are not provided. On the other hand, the $.pintan attribute has a default value that will pop up when you nullify (assigning to Nil) its value through its accessor. The DEPRECATED method will print a message to a standard error indicating the name of the method and that it has "seen" an instance of deprecated code.

The export trait is extremely important in modules. It effectively tells the compiler which routines are going to be *seen* outside the scope of the package, once it's loaded somewhere else:

```
package Moves {
    sub shuffle( *@deck ) is export {
        @deck.pick: *;
    }
}
import Moves;
say shuffle( "As de bastos", "3 de oros", "Sota de espadas" );
```

This program will print a shuffled version of the arguments to shuffle every time it's called. The important part is highlighted in boldface. You are using package as a generic wrapping for a single function; you could use class, module, or grammar and it would, in this case, have no effect. It would behave in the same way, simply creating a namespace where shuffle will reside and be isolated from another shuffle that could live in another package. With is export you signal it as an exportable routine. Later on, import is going to be used simply to import the symbols inside Moves into the current, main namespace, so that you can use shuffle directly, as you do in the next line. Please note that import does not work with external files; it needs as an argument an existing package. This command, however, may help you import selectively from a package:

```
package Moves {
    sub shuffle( *@deck ) is export(:shfl) {
        @deck.pick: *;
    }
    sub card-sort( *@deck ) is export {
        @deck.sort;
    }
}
```

```
import Moves :shfl;
say shuffle( "As de bastos", "3 de oros", "Sota de espadas" );
# say card-sort(<1♠ 5♣ 3♥>); # Purposefully commented out
```

In this case, you have added an argument to export. It's actually a Pair, shfl => True, but it will be a kind of tag or group for selective import. When you use it behind the name of the package you are importing from, it effectively says that you are interested in importing *only* routines with that tag. This also excludes that routine from the :DEFAULT group, which is the one that gets added when export is used with no arguments; in this case,

```
import Moves;
```

would only import card-sort, since shuffle is not in the :DEFAULT group. You need to add this group explicitly to the list in case you want it *also* to be exported by default:

```
sub shuffle( *@deck ) is export(:shfl :DEFAULT) {
    @deck.pick: *;
}
```

Other routines are ignored; cart-sort is commented out because it would cause an error if it was used. You can use the special tag :ALL to import all and everything:

```
import Moves :ALL;
```

This will import the two subroutines, and you'll be able to use them (by deleting the comment, obviously).

Working with Modules in External Files

Once you know how to declare *and* importing symbol works, you can split the programs into two or more different files. Strictly speaking, need is the keyword used to load compunits at compile time. The compunit loaded will be the one, found in the search path, that has the indicated argument as file name. You'll move your Moves package to a file named Moves.pm6 and use it with this program:

```
need Moves;
import Moves;
say shuffle( "As de bastos", "3 de oros", "Sota de espadas" );
say card-sort(<1♠ 5♣ 3♥>);
```

However, if you run this directly with perl6 need-package.p6, it is not going to work, with Perl 6 indicating

```
Could not find module Moves to import symbols from
```

Please note that this error is produced in the import sentence, not in need. The reason why this happens is that the compiler notices *first* that package does not exist before reporting that it does not because it didn't find it. So it's not that need is correct in this case, it's only that it's reported (and bailed out) before it even got the time to indicate the reason why that happens.

You need to understand first how compunit inclusion works in Perl 6. As in many other languages, there's a search path where modules are placed when installed. That search path also includes the directories where all the system class and modules reside. It generally does not include the current directory, which is indicated by "." in major operating systems. That's only logical and a security measure, but it makes your programs unable to find packages in the same directory, as in this case.

One way to fix it is to use the -I command line flag:

```
perl6 -I. need-package.p6
```

-I, followed by a directory name, will add that directory to the search path. Since Moves.pm6 is in the same directory as that file, this will be enough to find the module, import it, and run the rest of the program. Using need is, thus, more or less the same as declaring the module in the same place; you still need to import the symbols into the current namespace. Since these two statements are often used together, they are combined in the use command,

```
use Moves;
```

which does exactly the same as the two commands together.

Since use combines need and import, it uses the same syntax to import selectively as import did, so

```
use Moves :shfl;
```

will just import shuffle, leaving the other routine in its own package. It can still be used from the main program, as long as it's declared as our; sub defaults to lexical scope and in this case it will never be *seen* outside the scope:

```
our sub card-sort( *@deck ) is export { # in Moves.pm6
    @deck.sort;
}
say Moves::card-sort(<1♠ 5♣ 3♥>); # in use-package.p6
```

However, all of them work in compile time; as was shown before, external modules are loaded before proceeding to run the program. Module names are, effectively, constant in the same sense constants were defined in the previous chapter: they are defined at compile time and do not change during the program execution.

You will define another package, Moves-Pro,

```
unit package Moves-Pro;

sub shuffle( *@deck ) is export {
    @deck.pick( * ).reverse;
}
```

which adds an additional twist to the shuffle by reversing it and deciding which one to use by flipping a coin:

```
my $module = Bool.pick?? "Moves" !! "Moves-Pro";
require ::($module);
say ::("$module")::EXPORT::DEFAULT::('&shuffle')( "As de
bastos", "3 de oros", "Sota de espadas" );
```

The $module variable will contain the name of the module to load and require will load it. If you use a constant, require is going to be no different from use except it will be working during program execution. But if it's a variable, you need to use *indirect lookup* via the double-colon prefix. Indirect lookup is a way of interpolating variables to generate symbol names. You can use it also to generate variable names on the fly:

```
sub shuffle-pro( *@deck ) {
    @deck.pick( * ).reverse;
}

sub shuffle( *@deck ) {
    @deck.pick( * );
}

my $shuffle = Bool.pick?? "shuffle" !! "shuffle-pro";

say &::($shuffle)( "As de bastos", "3 de oros", "Sota de
espadas" );>
```

You will keep the name of the routine you are going to call in the variable $shuffle. You will break down indirect lookup of the variable name, which looks like this: &::($shuffle). First, the sigil indicates it's going to be a routine. The double colon then shows your intention to look up a name. You need the parentheses to indicate that you are going to use a variable or, in general, any expression to generate the variable name. For instance, taking into account that part of the name is shared, you could have used

```
my $pro = Bool.pick?? "" !! "-pro";
say &::("shuffle$pro")( "As de bastos", "3 de oros", "Sota de
espadas" );
```

You can even include the sigil in the part you are looking up, as in

```
say ::("\&shuffle$pro")( "As de bastos", "3 de oros", "Sota de
espadas" );
```

where you are taking care of escaping the sigil, since it's within an interpolating quote (""), which would understand it as a routine call otherwise.

The indirect lookup works in the same way, generating one name or the other. You are ready now to break down the routine name, as included by require:

- ::("$module") will resolve to a symbol, which will be the module name.

- ::EXPORT::DEFAULT accesses the table of exported routines in the DEFAULT group.

- Finally, ::('&shuffle') will look to return the symbol you are looking for. Please note the single quotes here.

These symbol tables are available for all modules loaded:

```
use Moves;
say Moves::EXPORT::.keys;     # (ALL DEFAULT shfl)
say Moves::EXPORT::DEFAULT::.keys; # (&shuffle &card-sort)
say &Moves::EXPORT::DEFAULT::shuffle( "As de bastos",
"3 de oros", "Sota de espadas" ); # Return the usual
```

The symbol table is a nested hash, and with .keys you can access its keys. The first level, EXPORT, will return the name of the hashes that contain the tags or groups to export. Every package will contain ALL and DEFAULT; this one (defined above) also includes shfl, which you have defined. Drilling down on the nested hashes, the DEFAULT hash will contain the names of the symbols, in this case routines, exported by default. By putting the sigil in front of the lookup and the name of the variable at the end, you can access it indirectly, although in this case it's been imported, so that long name is exactly equivalent to just using shuffle.

The first time a module is loaded, it's *precompiled*. This means that it's converted to a virtual machine format that can be used directly the next time it's run; these files are stored in a directory called .precomp, relative to where the program is being run. These directories and the files are managed by Perl 6, and you don't need to do anything about them. No problem if you delete them either, although it might take a bit longer to run the program because they will be regenerated when you do.

Pragmas

Pragmas are file-level directives used by Perl 6 to activate certain features or interpret the rest of the file in a certain way. They are activated by use and employ the same syntax as the inclusion of external modules.

You have already seen one: use v6, which is actually ignored by Perl 6 and is rather devoted to telling the Perl 5 interpreter this is not its turf. However, there are many more; see Table 10-2.

Table 10-2. *Most frequent pragmas*

Pragma	Arguments	Meaning
v6.c, v6.d		It indicates the minimum version the rest of the script should work with. Will error if the interpreter does not reach it.
MONKEY-SEE-NO-EVAL		Enables the use of the EVAL function.
lib	List with directories	Adds them to the search path.
soft		Enables the wrap function.
strict		Requires declaration of variables before using them. Enabled by default.
worries		Shows compile-time warnings. Enabled by default.
variables	:D	Forces definition of variables when they are declared.

The flip side of use is no: it disables a pragma.

```
no strict;
$totally-new-variable = 7
```

This will not produce any kind of error, despite not having declared the (by default compulsory) scope of $totally-new-variable.

The use lib pragma is interesting and will allow you to work with modules in the same directory without needing to give special flags to Perl 6:

```
use lib <.>;
require draw-two-cu <&draw-two>;
say draw-two;
```

This can be run with the default perl6 draw-2-require.p6. Besides, you are using it on this file,

```
sub draw-two( --> Slip ) is export {
    state @deck = 1..10 X <♠ ♦ ♣ ♥>;
    if @deck {
        my @shuffle = @deck.pick: *;
        my Slip $draw = (@shuffle.pop, @shuffle.pop).Slip;
        @deck = @shuffle;
        return $draw;
    } else {
        return [].Slip;
    }

}

say "loaded";
```

which does not declare any kind of module, although it does declare draw-two with the trait of export. Since no package is explicitly declared, you can't use tags to group routines. In that case, using the routine name itself (&draw-two) will include it in the current namespace, as shown by its execution.

Bear in mind that the directories are relative to the path the program is being executed; that is, Perl 6 will search exclusively in the directory where the program is run in this case, not in the directory relative to where the program script *is*. If you run it from another directory, it will not find the external file. In that case, you need to add to the list of directories all directories relative to where it could possibly be executed. In this case:

```
use lib <. Chapter10>;
```

This way, you will be able to run it from the same directory and the directory above without errors.

```
perl6 Chapter10/draw-2-require.p6
```

in this case.

The Perl 6 Ecosystem

Perl 6 has a rich ecosystem, including more than 2,000 modules at the time of this writing, with new versions and modules being added to it every day. The most important, or used, modules and classes are included in the Rakudo Star distribution, which is the one advised to most users. You'll see them next.

Rakudo Star Modules

The Rakudo Star modules are selected by the release managers so that developers using this distribution will be able to cover many needs without needing to download any additional module. The whole list is at `https://github.com/rakudo/star/blob/master/modules/MODULES.txt` and it includes, at the time of writing, around 60 modules.

A set of modules, for instance, is devoted to deal with JSON. These include JSON::Fast, JSON::Marshal, JSON::Unmarshal, JSON::Name, and JSON::Class. JSON is nowadays the standard for serialization of data structures, and is also extensively used for configuration files. It's very likely that you will need to write something like this in a program:

```
use JSON::Fast;
say to-json { 3 => '♠', 8 => '♣' };
```

You can use it directly if your distribution is Rakudo Star. You will obviously need to install it the way you will see in the next section if it is not. This will print a JSON representation of the hash, such as this one:

```
{
  "8": "♣",
  "3": "♠"
}
```

The order of the keys in the JSON file, as well as in any way you handle a hash, is never guaranteed. This is a security feature that was implemented in 2018.

Besides to-json, this module implements from-json; the Fast in its name indicates its intention.

A few other modules have the Web as a target and can be used to download content from the Web easily. Among them are LWP::Simple, WWW, and HTTP::UserAgent. The two first are simple clients; the last is a bit more complex and allows for more configuration of the client to create complex web clients and interactions with APIs. The URI module also checks and creates uniform resource locators from its parts.

You can create, for instance, an easy client to a random card generating API:

```
constant URL='https://deckofcardsapi.com/api/deck/';
use WWW;
my $deck-id = jget(URL ~ 'new/shuffle/?deck_count=1')<deck_id>;
say   jget URL ~ "/$deck-id/draw/?count=2";
```

This API, whose documentation is available at the domain above, generates random decks from which you can then start to draw cards. You use a single WWW command, `jget`, which downloads the content of an URL *and* decodes it from JSON. Since that's the format the API returns the data in, with a single command you retrieve the deck ID of the random deck that has been generated for you. You use that variable to retrieve two cards from another URL, which you print directly after the last statement in the program. Equivalently, WWW will include the rest of the HTTP commands `put` and `post`, preceded by j if you are using JSON.

While these modules are first thoroughly tested and then quite useful for simple programs, you will probably need, sooner or later, to use one of the modules from the ecosystem.

Ecosystem Modules

Most programming languages include a standard way of publishing open source libraries, and let anyone download them through a simple command line program. The modules can all be found at `https://modules.perl6.org`, but they reside in one of two places:

- CPAN is the Comprehensive Perl Archive Network, a place where authors can upload their open source modules. CPAN is shared with Perl 5; you need to be authorized to upload your modules there.

- Any open repository such as GitHub, and less commonly GitLab and BitBucket. In this case, authors simply add the metadata for their module to a list that resides in a GitHub repo.

The place where a module resides is (mostly) transparent. The way to install these modules is via the zef command-line interface.

Zef already comes installed with Rakudo Star, but you can also install it (or upgrade it) via rakudobrew using `rakudobrew build zef`, or by cloning the repository and then, once in it, typing

```
perl6 -I. bin/zef install .
```

As you might remember from above, this uses the same directory (.) to search for modules, and then runs a binary (`bin/zef`) with the arguments `install` and `.` so you are basically self-installing zef using zef.

Two commands are the ones you are most likely to use from zef.

```
zef search web
```

will search the ecosystem *and* CPAN for any module that includes web in its name; it will also include any modules that are already installed. See Figure 10-1.

```
===> Found 65 results
--------------------------------------------------------------------------------------------------
ID|From                                |Package                                        |Descript...
--------------------------------------------------------------------------------------------------
0 |Zef::Repository::Ecosystems<cpan>|WebService::Discourse:ver<0.1.0>:auth<github:azawawi>    |Use Disc.
1 |Zef::Repository::Ecosystems<cpan>|WebService::AWS::S3:ver<0.0.1>:auth<github:bduggan>       |AWS S3 C...
2 |Zef::Repository::Ecosystems<cpan>|WebService::AWS::S3:ver<0.0.2>:auth<github:bduggan>       |AWS S3 C...
3 |Zef::Repository::Ecosystems<cpan>|CamelPub:ver<0.1.0>                                       |Interact ..
4 |Zef::Repository::Ecosystems<cpan>|CamelPub:ver<0.2.0>                                       |Interact ..
5 |Zef::Repository::Ecosystems<cpan>|CamelPub:ver<0.2.5>                                       |Interact ..
6 |Zef::Repository::Ecosystems<cpan>|CamelPub:ver<0.2.6>                                       |Interact ..
7 |Zef::Repository::Ecosystems<cpan>|Cofra:ver<0.0.1>:auth<github:zostay>                      |Common o...
8 |Zef::Repository::Ecosystems<cpan>|Cofra:ver<0.0.2>:auth<github:zostay>                      |Common o...
9 |Zef::Repository::Ecosystems<cpan>|Cro::WebSocket:ver<0.7.1>                                 |Libraries .
```

Figure 10-1. *Result of zef search web, with the four columns*

The first time this is issued during a session it will take some time to download the updated indices of CPAN and the ecosystem. Depending on network (and server) status, this might take a while. You can update the index if you write `zef search –update`.

The main result here is in the column Package. From will say where it was obtained: locally (it will indicate LocalCache), from cpan (cpan), or the Perl6 ecosystem (p6c). However, as you see, the description is clipped.

You might get more information there (or filter it using the utility grep). If you want the full description, use

```
zef search web -- wrap
```

which will flesh out the Description column to include the full description.

Once you've found what you want with zef or via modules.perl6.org, you can install the distribution (which will include several modules) by using install, as in

```
zef install Cro::HTTP
```

for instance. This will install not only this module, but all the upstream dependencies that will be defined in its configuration. Depending again on the state of the network and the number of dependencies, this might take some time (and it positively will in this case, since it's a complex module with lots of dependencies). If it's already installed, and the version in the distribution location matches your local version, it will say so and refuse to install it unless you issue a -- force flag.

Once the distributions are installed, they will have created what is called by Perl 6 a repository in a specific location. They will automatically be added to the library search path, so that you only need to use them to get them into your program:

```
use lib <. Chapter10>;
use Cro::HTTP::Router;
use Cro::HTTP::Server;
use JSON::Fast;
use Draw-Two;
my $application = route {
    get -> 'cards' {
        content 'application/json', to-json draw-two;
    }
}
```

```
my Cro::Service $croupier = Cro::HTTP::Server.new:
    :host<localhost>, :port<31415>, :$application;
$croupier.start;
say "Server started";
react whenever signal(SIGINT) { $croupier.stop; exit; }
```

You are using several modules that are incorporated into the Cro::HTTP distro: Cro::HTTP::Router and Cro::HTTP::Server. The other classes (Cro::Service, for instance), are incorporated automatically. You are also using the JSON::Fast library mentioned before, and your very own Draw-Two module. The use lib at the beginning accounts for the directories this module might reside in.

In this compact program, you describe a route using Cro::HTTP::Router's command route, and then proceed to declare a service that will be effectively the server; it will listen in port 31415 and will only respond to localhost requests.

The react statement at the end of the program is needed to shut it down, but is also a concurrent feature of Perl 6. Cro is an excellent tool for creating concurrent, distributed applications.

You can access this API directly from the browser by typing http://localhost:31415/cards once it's started (it will print "Server started") or using curl/wget or other CLI client. See Figure 10-2.

```
perl6-quick-reference-apress [master●●] % perl6 Chapter10/card-server.p6 &
[2] 32236
perl6-quick-reference-apress [master●●] % Server started
curl http://localhost:31415/cards
[
    "5♣",
    "1♦"
]%
perl6-quick-reference-apress [master●●] % ▮
```

Figure 10-2. *Consuming the Cro API from the command line, after starting the application, via curl*

Every call will return a different couple of cards, until the deck is totally exhausted.

Concluding Remarks

This chapter set you on a journey that has gone from the syntax of modules in Perl 6 to the gates of the rich Perl 6 module ecosystem. Along the way, you have learned about traits and how important they are in the precise description of routine signatures and container properties.

You are now ready to create your own modularized application. In these cases, something might (and will) go wrong. In the next chapter, you will see how to react to runtime errors and how to address them programmatically.

CHAPTER 11

Errors and How to Work with Them

When Perl 6 Finds It Difficult to Understand What You Mean

As indicated in the first chapters, *error* is a very bad name for something that is, in general, a misunderstanding between the developer and the computer, or sometimes the user and the computer. It's simply a strict way of throwing up virtual hands and saying, "Well, I fail to see what you mean."

Since errors are simply a way of communicating something, there are many ways to work with, and sometimes around, them. Languages have some established mechanisms to do so. Most problems, however, arise from interaction with the user running the program. As is usual in this language, there are many ways to do that.

© J.J. Merelo 2019
J.J. Merelo, *Perl 6 Quick Syntax Reference*, https://doi.org/10.1007/978-1-4842-4956-7_11

Command Line Arguments

Let's first define a small module that you are going to use from several *main* programs, Deck:

```
unit class Deck;
has @.cards = 1..10 X~ <♠ ♦ ♣ ♥>;
method !_shuffle {
    @!cards = @!cards.pick: *;
}
submethod TWEAK {
    self!_shuffle;
}
method draw ( UInt $how-many = 1 --> Slip ) {
    if @!cards {
        self!_shuffle;
        my @draw = gather {
            for ^$how-many {
                take @!cards.pop
            }
        }
        return @draw.Slip;
    } else {
        return [].Slip;
    }
}
```

This program introduces a new syntax concept: the submethod TWEAK, which is a function that is called *after* the object has been built, but before it's returned (by new) to the user. You will always need to shuffle the deck, which is either generated automatically as a default or entered by the user. You will do it from this small program, for starters:

```
use Deck;
my Deck $this-deck .= new;
say "One card ", $this-deck.draw;
say "Three cards ", $this-deck.draw( 3 ).join(" 🂤 ");
```

Please remember that in this chapter and the upcoming ones, use lib <. directory-with-module> is assumed at the beginning of every script.

This program creates an instance of Deck and draws some cards from it. Let's make the user decide how many cards will be drawn:

The line use Deck will be assumed at the beginning of every script in the rest of the chapter unless noted otherwise.

```
my Deck $this-deck .= new;
my UInt $how-many = (@*ARGS[0] // 1).UInt;
say "Cards ", $this-deck.draw( $how-many ).join(" 🂤 ");
```

In this case, you use the *dynamic variable* @*ARGS, which contains an array of strings that have been used in the command line. If you call this with

```
% perl6 Chapter11-notest/use-deck-args.p6 3
```

then @*ARGS[0] will contain "3" as a string. This is why you need to turn it into something sensible by using (@*ARGS[0] // 1).Uint. The draw method uses either nothing (and will default to 1) or an Uint. // is the *defined-or* operator: if it's defined, it returns the value to the left; if it's not, it returns the value to the right. It's a nice, and idiomatic, way of assigning default values to variables. With no argument, it will default to 1.

177

@*ARGS is an example of dynamic variables, or more precisely, dynamic scope variables, all of which use the * twigil. Variables that might get a value depending on the program or compiler environment, or how it is run, are all dynamic variables. These variables are similar to global variables, since they are defined outside the lexical scope of a block (in this case, in Perl 6 itself), but global variables are visible in any inner block, while dynamic variables are visible in any block *called from* the block where the dynamic variable is defined. Even if they are undefined (as is the case here), using them will not result in an error.

Table 11-1 includes a quick reference to the most useful variables and what they contain.

Table 11-1. *Most useful dynamic variables and what they hold*

Variable	Content
%*ENV	Shell environment variable.
$*CWD	Directory the program is launched from.
$*DISTRO	Information about the operating system and version the program is running.
$*PERL	Version of Perl 6. Useful for reporting errors.
$*PROGRAM-NAME	Path to current executable.
$*COLLATION	Related to Unicode-enabled sorting.

The main problem here is that you get arguments as strings so you need to make some conversions. Besides, this assumes that you can access the command line. In some cases, that information might be available somewhere else, like environment variables.

Environment variables are defined from the command line using a variety of mechanisms that depend on the operating system and the shell you are using. In Linux, you would type export VARIABLE_ NAME=variablevalue in the most popular shells. In many cases, including deployment to the cloud, they will be predefined.

But you can also use environment variables. For instance, you used a fixed port to start the Cro server in the previous chapter. You could change it thus:

```
my Cro::Service $croupier = Cro::HTTP::Server.new:
    :host<localhost>, :port(%*ENV<CRO_PORT>), :$application;
$croupier.start;
say "Server started at %*ENV<CRO_PORT>";
```

Then you would define

```
export CRO_PORT=7777
```

and run it as before; the value of %*ENV<CRO_PORT> will be as defined. There's a good thing about this variable: it uses allomorphs instead of strings.

```
my Deck $this-deck .= new;
my $how-many = %*ENV<HOW_MANY> // 1;
say "Cards ", $this-deck.draw( $how-many ).join(" ♣ ");
```

This program looks the same as before, except for the fact that you don't need to convert the value of the environment variable. Since it's an allomorph (I talked about them in Chapter 3), it will behave as a number of as a string as required.

There is a limited amount of data you can enter this way. For instance, it's complicated to enter command-line flags or arguments of the kind –variable=value. Perl 6 does have a mechanism to deal with this: the MAIN sub:

```
sub MAIN( $how-many = 1) {
    my Deck $this-deck .= new;
    say "Cards ", $this-deck.draw( $how-many ).join(" ♥ ");
}
```

The MAIN routine is the one that is going to be called when running this script from the command line. You have switched from using dynamic variables to using all the power that comes with Signatures: default values, and also duck-typing of $how-many to the type you need it. Since this Signature uses a single Positional argument, the Positional arguments used when you run the program (same command lines as previously, with an optional number following the program name) are automatically bound to the variables you declare in the Signature. But, again, all the power of routines and Signatures is there with you.

```
my Deck $this-deck .= new;
multi sub MAIN() {
    say "Your card ", $this-deck.draw;
}
multi sub MAIN( $how-many ) {
    say "Cards ", $this-deck.draw( $how-many ).join(" ♥ ");
}
```

In this case, you declare $this-deck as a lexical variable that will be seen in the two multi MAINs. One of them will run when there's no argument, the other (with different message) when there's some value. See Figure 11-1.

```
perl6-quick-reference-apress [master] % perl6 Chapter11/multi-main.p6
Your card 6♦
perl6-quick-reference-apress [master●] % perl6 Chapter11/multi-main.p6 3
Cards 10♣ ♥ 7♦ ♥ 5♦
```

Figure 11-1. *Running the program with different arguments, making different MAINs kick in*

By turning MAIN into a multi, you can run different code depending on the input and even type-check:

```
multi sub MAIN( UInt $how-many ) {
    say "Cards ", $this-deck.draw( $how-many ).join(" 🂱 ");
}
```

In this case, if you run it with an argument that is not a number, an exception will occur and it will print

```
Usage:
  Chapter11/multi-main-type.p6
  Chapter11/multi-main-type.p6 <how-many>
```

This usage message is generated automatically by Perl 6 from the signatures of the MAIN subs. You can use it easily to also declare named parameters and even aliases.

Exceptions in the invocation parameters can be easily caught in the command line or by the signature mechanism of the MAIN sub. However, there might be some more complicated ones you will have to deal with within your program. In the rest of the chapter, you will see how Perl 6 does this.

Failures and Exceptions

An exception is something unexpected. Something that shouldn't have happened has happened, generally in connection with the exterior of the program: a non-existing file or 404-ed URL, a document with the wrong format. A program can't just stop working: it needs to address this error and move on. In general, in this case it will throw an exception. For instance, this program,

```
use JSON::Fast;
say from-json "foobar; baz";
```

will fail, The output will indicating something to the tune of that string not being correct JSON, which it is not. The first thing you might have noticed is that the error is printed even if you redirect standard output. So

```
perl6 exception-config.p6 > /tmp/foo
```

will still produce the same text even if you have redirected standard output with >, since that message is going to be printed in the standard error output, not standard output. In general, exceptions will be printed to that device, which by default is the same console.

You can also produce this kind of error yourself:

```
my $this-deck = Deck.new( cards => ( <A J Q K> X~ <♠ ♦ ♣ ♥> ) );
multi sub MAIN( UInt $how-many ) {
    die "There aren't that many cards" if $how-many > 16;
    say "Cards ", $this-deck.draw( $how-many ).join(" ♟ ");
}
```

die produces an exception, which effectively, if nothing is done about it, exits the program, printing the message in standard error output:

```
There aren't that many cards
  in sub MAIN at Chapter11/die.p6 line 15
  in block <unit> at Chapter11/die.p6 line 8
```

What die does is create an exception. Exceptions indicate something is wrong and they have information about what has produced them. Exception is also the base class for a host of standard and ad-hoc exception classes, all of which have the form X::Namespace::SpecificException.

However, this exception is unspecific. In a strongly typed language, exceptions need to have a particular type.

```
if $how-many > 16 {
    X::Numeric::Overflow.new.throw ;
}
```

All exceptions use the X:: namespace, with a secondary namespace with the type of exception and a final part that specifies the particular type of exception. In this case, you have used "Overflow", which is related to using a size bigger than is possible or available. The main secondary exception types are included in Table 11-2.

Table 11-2. *Main secondary exception types*

Exception type	Context or application
OS	Operating system errors
ControlFlow	Occurs in the context of deciding what to do next in a data structure
Control	Exceptions occurred during execution of control structures; X::Control is abbreviated to CX
SecurityPolicy	In EVAL functions
AdHoc	Used when no other type fits
Dynamic	Used for dynamic variables
Method	Used for methods
Role	When creating roles
Pragma	For pragmas
IO	Input/Output
NYI	Not yet implemented
OutOfRange	Off appropriate Range

There are several hundred default exception types, with some conventions that appear throughout all of them (for instance, NotFound or Unknown). So far, just a few of them are documented. Their usage, however, is conventional and you're free to use them any way you

want and deal with them the way you need. For instance, you can use
X::OutOfRange in the example above instead of the chosen one. This is
what you will see in the next section.

This program is also dealing with an exception that should be dealt
with at another level. As a matter of fact, the module itself should take care
of whatever problems arise. The problem is that throwing an exception
from inside the module does not give anyone the chance to actually deal
with it. Enter *failures*. Failures wrap around exceptions, and they give the
developer the chance to work with them or to check them before throwing
an error. Let's modify the Deck you used before, changing the method to
this in Decker:

```
method draw ( UInt $how-many = 1 ) {
    if ( $how-many > @!cards.elems ) {
      return X::OutOfRange.new( got => $how-many,
                               range => "1.." ~ @!cards.elems).fail
    }
    if @!cards {
        self!_shuffle;
        my @draw = gather {
            for ^$how-many {
                take @!cards.pop
            }
        }
        return @draw.Slip;
    } else {
        return X::OutOfRange.new.fail;
    }
}
```

You are actually using X::OutOfRange with its instance variables
initialized to indicate what you have and how it's outside the Range. But
that will create an exception, so you call .fail to create a failure out of it.

You actually return that failure from the method, which you have modified, eliminating the return constraint, so that it can return either a Slip or a failure.

If you call it from here with number 44,

```
my Decker $this-deck .= new;
my UInt $how-many = (@*ARGS[0] // 1).UInt;
say "Cards ", $this-deck.draw( $how-many ).join(" ♥ ");
```

it will produce this error:

```
Argument out of range. Is: 44, should be in 1..40
```

The error message is composed by the exception from its attributes. When you actually try to use a failure, it will throw the exception it hosts. In that sense, it's not buying you much other than the fact that you're dealing with the problem where it happens. However, the interesting thing about failures is that you can avoid that by actually dealing with them. You'll see how in the next section.

Dealing with Errors

An error in the shape of an exception or failure does not mean the program should stop. You can deal with them, if only to inform the user or coder; you can even retry or recover from them if possible if you know what you are dealing with. Dealing with failures can be done by checking for definedness of the variable. Since failure is a subclass of Nil, it will not be defined, unlike a proper variable returned by a routine, which will always be defined:

```
my Decker $this-deck .= new;
```

```
my $draw = $this-deck.draw: (@*ARGS[0] // 1).UInt;
```

```
if $draw.defined == False {
    say "Oops, something went wrong →\n\t", $draw.exception;
} else {
    say "Cards ",  $draw.join(" 🌷 ");
}
```

You know that $draw will contain either the return value or a failure. You then check if it's not defined, that is, if $draw.defined is False. In that case, you know it's a failure and that it's wrapping an exception, which you extract calling .exception on it. That exception will stringify to the exception message, printing something like this (for an argument of 44):

```
Oops, something went wrong →
Argument out of range. Is: 44, should be in 1..40
```

This way, you are effectively dealing with the original exception, using your own error message in this case; you could also do a more argument-appropriate action like using a default value.

In general, we talk about throwing an exception and *catching* it when we deal with it. Exceptions can be caught at any level, but we usually try to catch them at the highest level. Let's try this new module called Deckeroo.pm6. Only this method will change:

```
method draw ( UInt $how-many = 1 --> Slip) {
    if ( ! @!cards.elems ) {
      X::AdHoc.new( payload => "No more cards" ).throw
    }
    if ( $how-many > @!cards.elems ) {
      X::OutOfRange.new( got => $how-many,
                    range => "1.." ~ @!cards.elems).throw
    }
    if @!cards {
        self!_shuffle;
```

```
    my @draw = gather {
        for ^$how-many {
            take @!cards.pop
        }
    }
    return @draw.Slip;
    }
}
```

You have two possible exceptions, one for which you will use AdHoc
and which states that you have run out of cards, and another when the
request is for more cards than there are in the deck. You have returned to
constrain the return value since, in case there's an exception, you will deal
with it not through the return value, but by catching it.

The main program will change to this:

```
use Deckeroo;
my Deckeroo $this-deck .= new;
CATCH {
    when X::AdHoc { .Str.say }
    when X::OutOfRange { say "We don't have that many cards: ",
    $_.Str; }
    default { say "Something has happened: $_"; }
}
for ^(@*ARGS[0] // 1) {
    say "Cards ", $this-deck.draw(( @*ARGS[1] // 2 ).UInt ).
    join(" ♣ ");
}
```

The CATCH block is similar to a given block: it will have different
options preceded by when, and a default option that will be run if none
of the others match. In this case, you have a clause for every one of the

two exceptions. Since when is a topicalizer, the actual exception will be included in the topic variable $_; you can print it directly (with .Str. say or say $_.Str) or simply interpolate it in your own message, thus wrapping it.

In this case, you are calling the program with two arguments, one for the number of draws and the other for the number of cards:

```
> perl6 catch.p6 7 4
Cards 9♦ 🤡 7♠ 🤡 4♦ 🤡 6♦
Cards 8♥ 🤡 5♥ 🤡 10♥ 🤡 5♠
Cards 2♥ 🤡 3♣ 🤡 4♥ 🤡 7♣
Cards 6♣ 🤡 10♣ 🤡 3♠ 🤡 8♠
Cards 1♣ 🤡 2♦ 🤡 5♦ 🤡 3♥
Cards 8♦ 🤡 1♦ 🤡 7♦ 🤡 6♥
Cards 10♦ 🤡 7♥ 🤡 1♠ 🤡 8♣
```

This output is correct, but different combinations will trigger exceptions that will be captured by the CATCH block. For instance,

```
perl6 catch.p6 11 4
Cards 10♥ 🤡 7♣ 🤡 3♠ 🤡 4♣
#...
No more cards
```

This is the first exception, triggered when you are calling the deck and it has no cards left.

```
>perl6 catch.p6 1 54
We don't have that many cards: Argument out of range. Is: 54,
should be in 1..40
```

In this case, it indicates the second argument is out of Range. Some unexpected error might occur, too:

```
>perl6 catch.p6 one 2
```

Something has happened: Cannot convert string to number:
base-10 number must begin with valid digits or '.' in '♠one'
(indicated by ♠)

In this case, the exception has occurred at the same level as the CATCH block. Since this was not foreseen, the default clause is activated.

You might also want to check if something is running or not, letting it through if it's OK, but just skipping it if it didn't work. The try blocks do precisely that: they run the code in them, dropping the exceptions if they occur.

Wrapping the previous code in a try block will achieve this effect:

```
try {
    for ^(@*ARGS[0] // 1) {
      say "Cards ",  $this-deck.draw(( @*ARGS[1] // 2 ).UInt ).
      join(" ♣ ");
    }
}
```

Running this code with the same options as before will work correctly if both arguments are OK and will simply do nothing if they are not. In the code above and in the following case, try can also be used as an statement prefix:

```
try for ^(@*ARGS[0] // 1) {
      say "Cards ",  $this-deck.draw(( @*ARGS[1] // 2 ).UInt ).
      join(" ♣ ");
}
```

Since the block contains only the for statement, the try preceding it will affect anything that happens within it.

To use X::AdHoc as an exception for your particular application is enough in most cases, but a better practice would be to create your own exception classes so that you can deal with them specifically. Your classes will have to subclass Exception:

```
unit class X::Cards::NoMore is Exception;

method message() {
        "No more cards left, sorry";
}
```

Not much more than the message method needs to be overridden. You will include it in your module (it's called Deckie this time):

```
use X::Cards::NoMore;
# @.cards, _shuffle and TWEAK defined as usual
method draw ( UInt $how-many = 1 --> Slip ) {
    if ( ! @!cards.elems ) {
      X::Cards::NoMore.new.throw
    }
    # Rest will remain the same
}
```

You can use it from your program in the same way as before. When draw is called repeatedly and the deck exhausted, the typed message will be thrown and, if uncaught, will print the specific message and exit.

Concluding Remarks

In this chapter, after showing the syntax for invoking a program using arguments in several possible ways, you have seen how exceptions and failures are produced, and also how to deal with them, including how to create your own exception classes for use in your programs.

Avoiding errors at another level includes testing your code extensively. You will see how to do that in the next chapter.

## CHAPTER 12

Interacting with the System

Working with the Filesystem, the Network, and Everything That's Out There

Interacting with the system is not nowadays as important as it was before. Where ten years ago most language references started with "hello world" and an Open file command, nowadays most programs run in environments where interaction is done through environment variables (which you saw in Chapter 11) or through the web (seen in Chapter 10). Still, knowing how to interact with the system is an integral part of many programs, even more so when we need to run applications written in other languages. You'll get to this next.

Running External Programs

Running external programs implies knowing their path and handling the command that runs the argument needed to get them going. And there are two distinct ways of doing this:

- **Through a kernel call**: The operating system kernel includes a group of functions that can run external programs with arguments.

© J.J. Merelo 2019
J.J. Merelo, *Perl 6 Quick Syntax Reference*, https://doi.org/10.1007/978-1-4842-4956-7_12

- **Through the shell**: These are higher level calls that run a shell and give it a program to run together with its arguments.

There are many differences between the former and the latter, but you can think of the latter as running a program the same way you would do it from the command line: taking into account environment variables and shell facilities such as shell expansion, internal commands (such as echo or cd in Linux shells), and filesystem navigation. Kernel calls, however, do not offer such facilities: you need, for instance, to include the full path to the program you are running, as well as the full list of arguments and the expanded environment variables.

Perl 6 includes different commands to run external programs using any of these methods. See Table 12-1.

Table 12-1. *Commands for running external processes*

Command	Type	Action
run	Kernel	Runs an external program with input and output redirection if needed.
Proc.new	Kernel	Creates an object that captures interaction with an external program
shell	Shell	Runs an external program using a predetermined shell, including redirection
qx, qqx	Shell	Quote construct that runs an external program

You are going to use a small game I released for this purpose, App::Game::Concentration. In this game, a deck of card is arranged randomly in four rows of 13 cards each. The player picks 2 cards, and they are eliminated if their pips (Ace, Jack, Queen, King, or number) are the same. If they are not, they are turned back again. The *concentration* in the name comes from the fact that you have to remember, once you get a particular card, where it was when a possible pair shows up in another selection.

Once the game has been installed with zef App::Game::Concentration, it can be run from the command line by typing concentration. It shows a prompt with the format the two card positions should be typed in: the one after the other separated by a single whitespace, row and column separated by comma. A blank line will finish the game. See Figure 12-1.

You can also download the game from the source, https://github.com/JJ/p6-app-concentration, and run it directly from there, just in case you want to hack it yourself.

```
App-Game-Concentration [master●] % perl6 -Ilib bin/concentration
row-1,column-1 row-2,column-2 » 1,1 2,3
K ♣-10 ♣
row-1,column-1 row-2,column-2 » 3,2 2,3
4 ♦-10 ♣
row-1,column-1 row-2,column-2 » 1,12 2,13
3 ♠-J ♥
row-1 column-1 row-2 column-2 » ▯
```

Figure 12-1. *Playing the concentration game from the command line*

The easiest way to play is to run it via the shell, because since it's installed, it will be in the path:

```
shell "concentration";
```

This will start the game and behave exactly in the same way as if you had run it from the command line (as seen in Figure 12-1): it will show the prompt and wait for your answer. You can run anything you could do from the command line, so this is also valid:

```
shell "echo '1,1 2,2' | concentration";
```

This will work in Linux, since echo is an internal shell command.

This command uses a pipe (|), which connects the standard output of the command to its left to the standard input of the command to its right. That is, it's as if echo was typing at the prompt of concentration. The output will be equivalent to typing a single line, and then a blank line, which will exit the program. Something like this:

```
row-1,column-1 row-2,column-2 » 6 ♥-J ♥
row-1,column-1 row-2,column-2 »
```

Your provided input does not show up in the command line; the two cards shown after the prompt will be the ones that will show in interactive mode under the prompt.

This also shows a way to control a program by grabbing its input and output. The shell command can be invoked with a number of named arguments that take this into account. The most important are shown in Table 12-2.

Table 12-2. *Named arguments for functions invoking external programs*

Argument	Default value	Description
:$in	'-'	Capture input
:$out	'-'	Capture output
:$err	'-'	Capture error output
:$bin		Binary (non-text) format
:$chomp	True	Eliminate carriage return
:$enc		Encoding
:$cwd	$*CWD	Directory the command will be run in
:$env		Environment variables

You can replicate the result of the above program with this one, which grabs the input stream of the program:

```
my $concentration = shell "concentration", :in;
$concentration.in.put("1,1 2,2");
```

The shell command returns a Proc. This is a type that has information on external processes; as a matter of fact, you can interact with the system via the constructor. Since you are going to create a pipe from your program to the external program you are running, this variable will include, among other things, that pipe. Using :in as an argument to shell indicates that you are going to set up an input stream from you to the program.

You can access that stream using the attribute in of the variable, which works like an input/output stream. You can write to it using put (also say and print). The output of this program, in this case, will be very similar to the previous one, except that you will notice that it exits *before* it prints the output (including the prompt and the result of this first selection).

The Proc objects have the attributes and methods shown in Table 12-3.

Table 12-3. *Attributes for Proc objects*

Method	Type	Description
in, out, err	IO::Pipe	Connection to the standard input, output, and error output of the process
exitcode		The process exit code once it's finished. 0 means exited successfully; default value is -1
pid		Process ID
command		The actual command it has run
shell		Starts a command using the shell

Creating a Proc initializes an object with a series of attributes you might need in several commands, but it also gives you the methods above to interact with the program:

```
my $concentration = Proc.new: :in :out;
$concentration.shell: "concentration";
$concentration.in.say("1,1 2,2");
$concentration.in.close;
say "Output is \n\t", $concentration.out.lines().join("\n\t");
```

You create a Proc object in the first line, and in this case you'll be grabbing input and output. This is an empty process, but you actually attach the game by calling the shell method. As you did before, you send data to standard input, but since you'll be interacting with standard output too, you need to close that stream. $concentration.out is another IO::Pipe from which, in this case, you read using lines. With this, you reformat the output slightly, printing it in this fashion:

```
Output is
        row-1,column-1 row-2,column-2 » K ♠-9 ♣
        row-1,column-1 row-2,column-2 »
```

But the interesting thing is that you can, this way, control input/output-bound console programs, interacting with them.

Using run is similar to using shell, except that, well, no shell is involved:

```
my $cal = run "cal", "1965", :out;
say "The whole calendar for 1965\n\n", $cal.out.lines().
join("\n\t");
```

You call run with the name of the program and the argument you want for it, 1965 in this case. You will capture output if only to frame it in a slightly different way. In the same way as it was done before, you will *read* the lines of the output of the command from the pipe and print them preceded by a tab stop. If you need to run programs with lower overhead and no use of shell functionalities, run might be a much better option.

Input and Output

The easiest way to work with files is to let Perl 6 open them for you. If you pass the name of several files (through, for instance, a glob) in the command line, the dynamic variable $*ARGFILES will let you directly access the content of the files:

```
if $*ARGFILES.path ~~ IO::Special {
    say "No input"
} else {
    $*ARGFILES.lines.elems.say
}
```

You can use this program this way:

```
perl6 argfiles.p6 *.p6
```

Without an argument, it will simply print "No input". $*ARGFILES is a magic variable that contains the collated content of all files that are supplied as arguments. Without them, $*ARGFILES will instead read from standard input and it will become a IO::Special handle pointing to STDIN, standard input. You are not interested in that behavior, so the program will simply exit with a message.

If that's not the case, .lines will return a list with all lines in the open file; .elems will count them, and say will print them.

Being as simple and straightforward as it is, $*ARGFILES gives you a hint on how input-output works in Perl 6. Classes for it are in the IO namespace. Table 12-4 lists the most important ones.

Table 12-4. *Most important IO classes and their superclasses*

Class	Is a	Description
IO::ArgFiles	IO::CatHandle	$*ARGFILES is an instance.
IO::Cathandle	IO::Handle	Single handle for multiple files.
IO::Handle		Object for a single input or output stream.
IO::Pipe	IO::Handle	Used for communication between your program and external programs.
IO::Special		Used for standard input, output and error output.
IO::Path	Cool	Used to store the path in a OS-independent way.

As is usual, you need to first specify a file to be opened before being able to work with it. The file will usually be described with a string, but you need to turn this string into a Path before being able to work with it.

IO::Path includes a series of tests for files, as well as other functionalities. The file tests are listed in Table 12-5.

Table 12-5. *File test methods*

Test	Description	Returns or throws
d	Directory?	True/False
e	Exists?	True/False
f	File?	True/X::IO::DoesNotExist
l	Symbolic link?	True/X::IO::DoesNotExist
r	Readable?	True/X::IO::DoesNotExist

(continued)

Table 12-5. (*continued*)

Test	Description	Returns or throws
rw	Readable and writable?	True/X::IO::DoesNotExist
rwx	Readable and writable and executable?	True/X::IO::DoesNotExist
s	Size in bytes	True/X::IO::DoesNotExist
w	Writable?	True/X::IO::DoesNotExist
x	Executable?	True/X::IO::DoesNotExist
z	Size is zero?	True/X::IO::DoesNotExist

For instance, you might use this script to check the directory where the file itself resides:

```
say <. Chapter12>.map:  { $_ => "$_/x.p6".IO.e };
```

This will print something like

```
(. => True Chapter12 => False)
```

if you run it from the same directory. .IO is a Cool function that returns an IO::Path, which, created on the fly, is checked for existence. In the case above, it's run from the same directory; if run from above, it would return the opposite.

You can chain several IO operations too:

```
say <. Chapter12>
    .map( * ~ "/x.p6")
    .grep( { .IO.e } )
    .map( { $_ => .IO.s } )
```

First you create the possible file names with map, then you filter with only the existing ones remaining, and finally you compute the size using the .s method. This will print (./x.p6 => 104) if you run it from the same directory.

You can already work with a file handle to extract information from it, or to write to it. Table 12-6 shows the main methods that can be used directly on a handle.

Table 12-6. *Methods for handles*

Method	Description
comb	Searches for occurrences of a string in the file
lines	Returns the sequence of lines in the file
words	Returns a sequence of words in the file
split	Splits the file by the given string and returns the resulting list
spurt	Writes the content of a variable or sets of variables to a file
print, say, put	Same behavior as routines, acting on the handle
slurp	Reads the whole file

These methods do not need to explicitly open or close the file.

```
"/tmp/cards.txt".IO.spurt: 1..10 X~ <♠ ♦ ♣ ♥>;
```

will print a deck of cards to the indicated file and close it. The following, on the other hand, will open, read it, and perform the comb operation, retrieving all hearts present in the file:

```
say "/tmp/cards.txt".IO.comb: "♥";
```

You will need to open and eventually close a file if you want to use more complex operations or specify special opening modes. Table 12-7 shows how to specify the opening mode in different ways.

Table 12-7. *Opening modes*

Mode	Description
r	Default mode, open for reading only
w	Write only
x	Will fail if the file exists
a	Adds to the end of the file
update	Read and write mode
rw	Same as above
rx	Read/write and exclusive mode
ra	Reads/write and append mode
create	Will create the file if it does not exist
append	Will append to the end of the file
truncate	The file will be overwritten if it exists
exclusive	Same as x
bin	Used for opening binary files
mode	ro == read only, wo == write only, rw == read/write

Single and two-letters modes can be combined among themselves or with the mo and long-word options; however, the results might be unpredictable and it's better to stick to one of the different modes.

```
my $open-first = "/tmp/cards.txt".IO.open: :mode<wo>;
$open-first.put: 1..10 X~ <♠ ♦ ♣ ♥>;
$open-first.close;
```

This will recreate the same file you had before, so in most cases if all data can be processed or written in a single pass, spurt/slurp are preferred. Opening, however, has more options and the whole list, besides opening modes, is shown in Table 12-8.

Table 12-8. *Additional options for opening files*

Argument	Default	Description
chomp	True	Removes newlines.
nl-out, nl-in	OS-dependent	Defines the characters that will be used for newline.
out-buffer	True	Creates an output buffer with a defined number of bytes, or disables using False. True will use the default implementation.
enc	utf8	Encoding for non-binary files.

For instance, you can work with binary files as shown in this script:

```
use LWP::Simple;
constant $filename = "/tmp/camelia.ico";
my $camelia = LWP::Simple.get( 'https://docs.perl6.org/
favicon.ico' );
my $binary-file = $filename.IO.open: :bin, :w;
$binary-file.write( $camelia );
$binary-file.close;
say "Written $filename";
```

This code will download from the documentation page the Camelia icon and write it to a file in the /tmp directory (please change it to a Windows equivalent in that case). You use LWP::Simple.get, which is not exported so you need to employ its fully qualified name to download the file and then open a file in binary and write-only mode, and write to it using the .write method, which is preferred to say|put|print in the case of binary content. Write works on Bufs (which you saw in Chapter 5); get will conveniently return a Buf in the case of binary content.

After closing the file handle, you can visualize the file using eog or any other utility. You can also read it in binary mode using read:

```
constant $filename = "/tmp/camelia.ico";
my $binary-file = $filename.IO.open: :bin, :r;
my $camelia = $binary-file.read;
$binary-file.close;
say "Read ", $camelia.elems, " bytes";
```

The read method can be qualified with a number of bytes; by default, it will read in 65536 bytes or the size of the file. Since $camelia is a Buf, the number of elements in it will correspond to the file size, at least in Linux. The last line will effectively print the same number of bytes as the one that would appear with ls.

Concluding Remarks

This chapter has shown the syntax of interactions with other programs in the system, as well as how to write and read files of different types, including binary files such as images.

A good program, however, can't be said to work unless it's thoroughly tested. Perl 6 includes a Test module as part of the core library. You'll learn about it in the next chapter.

CHAPTER 13

Testing Your Modules and Scripts

If It's not Tested, It's Broken

Testing is so fundamental for software development nowadays that most languages include at least some basic testing capability in their standard libraries. This usually comes in the form of unit testing libraries: unit tests check how individual functions behave, what they return, and how they change the global or local state.

In the case of Perl 6, the standard testing library is simply called Test.

The Standard Testing Module: Test

Test is a standard module, but it is not part of the core, so you need to use it to incorporate it into your tests. It's generally used only within test programs, and they conventionally get the .t extension, instead of the usual .p6.

```
use Test;
sub returns-forty-two( --> 42 ) {};
is( returns-forty-two, 42, "Returns 42");
```

© J.J. Merelo 2019
J.J. Merelo, *Perl 6 Quick Syntax Reference*, https://doi.org/10.1007/978-1-4842-4956-7_13

Here you are testing a subroutine that always returns 42, and you check that it does so every time. You use a typical test command, is. Most testing commands are of the form

```
type of test( obtained-result, required-result, test-description)
```

And the code above will return

```
ok 1 - Returns 42
```

which is also of the form

```
(ok or not ok)  (test number ) - (Test message)
```

From now on, I'll omit the use Test line for brevity.

If it fails, the output will be of a different form.

```
sub returns-forty-two( --> 42 ) {};
ok( returns-forty-two() == 66, "Returns 42");
```

In this case, it will print

```
not ok 1 - Returns 42
# Failed test 'Returns 42'
# at ../Chapter13-notest/not-ok.p6 line 9
```

Here you are using ok instead of is. While is checks for equality, ok simply checks that the expression as first argument is truish, that is, can be reduced to True.

There are other tests available, as shown in Table 13-1.

Table 13-1. *Test functions*

Test	Description
ok, nok	The first argument is truish or false-ish.
is, isnt	The first argument is eq (for objects) or === (for type objects); it's negated in the second case.
is-approx	The difference in numeric value is smaller than a preset threshold.
is-deeply	When compared using eqv, the result is True.
cmp-ok	The first and third argument are compared using the operator that is the second argument.
isa-ok	Checks if the first argument is of the class passed as the second.
can-ok	Checks if an object has the method that is the second argument. This is passed as a string.
does-ok	Checks if a variable does a role.
like, unlike	Compares using regular expressions.
use-ok	A module can be used without throwing an exception.
dies-ok, lives-ok	Checks if the code throws, or does not throw, exceptions.
eval-dies-ok, eval-lives-ok	Checks if a string that's going to be evaluated throws, or not, exceptions.
throws-like, fails-like	Checks that it throws an exception or returns a failure as expected.

Trying and using it is something you should do with every module before running any other test:

```
plan 1;
use-ok( "Deckie", "Can use library");
```

This will return

```
1..1
ok 1 - Can use library
```

which adds, at the beginning, the testing "plan" outlined. In this case, you have indicated that you are going to be running a single file via Test's plan command. By the end of the program, Test will complain if you have run a different number of tests this way:

```
1..2
ok 1 - Can use library
# Looks like you planned 2 tests, but ran 1
```

It's convenient to say the tests you intend to run, but if that number is variable or you want to simply indicate testing has finished, there's another option:

```
use Deckie;
my $deck = Deckie.new;
for 1..($deck.cards.elems/2) {
    my $draw = $deck.draw( 2 );
    is( $draw.elems, 2, "Correct number of elems" );
    cmp-ok( +$draw.comb[0], ">", 0, "Figure OK");
}
throws-like { $deck.draw( 2 ) }, X::Cards::NoMore, "No more
cards" ;
done-testing;
```

This will test every functionality of the class you created in Chapter 11. You're testing if the draw returns the right number of elements, and also if the first one is a number. But that module throws exceptions, and they must be tested too. You can use throws-like, but in this case you have to use a block, not a call; throws-like will capture the exception and check it. This test will return something like

```
ok 1 - Correct number of elems
ok 2 - Figure OK
[...]
ok 40 - Figure OK
    1..2
    ok 1 - code dies
    ok 2 - right exception type (X::Cards::NoMore)
ok 41 - No more cards
1..41
```

which is first a subtest that checks that the code does thrown an exception and that it is the correct type, and if those are both OK, it will show the message "No more cards". In this case, where you are using done-testing for indicating the end of the tests, the number of tests will be shown at the end of the testing script, not at the beginning as it did before.

You can precede the tests with plan *, but it will have more or less the same effect. Also, when two tests are related or applied to the same object, you can group them in subtests:

```
plan *;
my $deck = Deckie.new;
for 1..($deck.cards.elems/2) {
    my $draw = $deck.draw( 2 );
```

```
subtest {
    is( $draw.elems, 2, "Correct number of elems" );
    cmp-ok( +$draw.comb[0], ">", 0, "Figure OK");
}, "Testing card hand"
}
```

This mainly has the effect of making subtests appear as a single test, so that if one of the tests fails, the whole subtest will fail too.

Several routines in this module are not really test functions, but can help describe them or provide functionality to selectively apply tests. They are described in Table 13-2.

Table 13-2. *Additional functions in the Test module*

Routine	Description
todo, skip, skip-rest	Takes $reason and $count as positional arguments; the next $count tests (or one) will be skipped for $reason. TODO will be printed in the first case. skip-rest skips whatever tests are left.
pass, flunk	Says via a message that a test has passed or not.
bail-out	Skips tests and exits with state 1.
diag	Displays a well-formatted message.

Other Testing Modules

The Test module contains everything that is needed for basic tests. However, it misses tests for complicated events or specific needs. This is why there are several modules in the ecosystem that can help you, most of them using the Test namespace. See Table 13-3.

Table 13-3. *Some useful Test modules*

Module	Description
Test::Output	Tests what is written to STDOUT and STDERR
Test::When	Runs only the groups of tests requested by the user, or selectively runs them based on the values of environment variables.
Test::Mock	Creates mock-ups of classes that can be checked for number of invocations and how these invocations are made.
Testo	Tests "done right," an alternative implementation of Perl 6 test functions.

This program, for instance, uses Testo to test the output of another program (the ok.p6 introduced earlier in this chapter):

```
plan 1;
my $path = "./ok.p6".IO.e??"./ok.p6"!!"Chapter13/ok.p6";
is-run $path, :out("ok 1 - Returns 42\n"), "Runs test";
```

This will return

```
1..1
    1..3
    ok 1 - STDOUT
    ok 2 - STDERR
    ok 3 - Status
ok 1 - Runs test
```

which indicates it is running three subtests checking for standard output and error as well as the exit status, and passes the single test if all three of them are correct.

You can use `Testo` if these are the kinds of things you want to test, or if you want to employ any of the other functions (such as `is-eqv`) that it adds to the standard Test.

Testing Best Practices

A test in Perl 6 is simply a program that uses the Test module. There are a series of conventions around testing that are generally respected:

- Tests are hosted in the `t/` directory and have the `.t` extension. Optional or author tests are placed in the `xt/` directory. They generally take a number, with `00-load.t` being the first, and it simply tests that the modules actually compile, and the rest going after that. You should number them in order of complexity, so that the simpler fail first and act as a canary in a mine, revealing errors early.

- Unitary tests should test every user-facing (i.e. not hidden) function and method, using argument combinations so that all possible branches are taken and tested and all possible outputs, including exceptions, are tested.

- Test everything, including stand-alone scripts. To do so, divide them into a module + script calling it, and test all possible combinations of arguments the script will receive, including variable values and so on.

Since tests are simply Perl 6 programs, you can run them as any other. However, when you have a set of tests, you usually need a script to run them; this script will usually hide the individual output of tests, yielding a report with the number of tests run and which ones have failed. For instance, let's place this program, deckie-subtests.t in a t/ directory hanging off the main one:

```
plan 20;
my $deck = Deckie.new;
for 1..($deck.cards.elems/2) {
    given $deck.draw( 2 ) {
        isnt( @_[0], @_[1], "Cards from pair are different");
    }
}
```

This program plans in advance how many tests you are going to have, so that an early stopping is indicated as failure.

You will need to install App::Prove6 in order to run the tests and get this report. This module implements an interpreter of the "Test anything protocol" (TAP), the simple text-based format used to report compliance or failure with tests. It will install the prove6 script, which you will run from the directory from which t hangs by simply typing prove6, obtaining this output:

```
t/deckie-subtests.t .. ok
All tests successful.
Files=1, Tests=20,  0 wallclock secs
Result: PASS
```

You should run tests automatically when you push to master. In order to do that, the best way is to sign up for some continuous integration system with a free tier for open source such as Travis CI. There is an official Perl 6 Travis configuration file, but I very much prefer mine, which is based on a Docker container and runs much faster, since it does not need to download and compile perl 6 before running the tests:

```
language:
  - minimal
```

```
services:
  - docker
install:
  - docker pull jjmerelo/test-perl6
script: docker run -t -v $TRAVIS_BUILD_DIR:/test jjmerelo/
test-perl6
```

This is a YAML file, which is conceptually similar to JSON but with a slightly different syntax. It's a series of key-value pairs, with the language, services, install and script keys, and arrays as values, with every array element preceded by a tab and a dash. Thus,

```
services:
  - docker
```

is declaring a pair with "services" as key and a value like ['docker']. These keys are interpreted in a sequence that is predefined and independent of how it appears in the file; the "minimal" language indicates you are not going to download any specific language, and the "docker" for services tells it to fire up the docker service. Once that's done, the "install" phase will download the jjmerelo/test-perl6 docker image. Testing will actually take place by running the value of the "script" key, which mounts via -v the current directory inside the image and simply runs the default test.

You will need to save this file as .travis.yml in the main module directory; you will obviously need to sign up for Travis and enable it in the repository you are running to get it going. Travis will run your tests for you and send you a message when the state of the result (PASS or FAIL) changes.

This module needs a META.json file to be present. The whole syntax of this file will be seen later. For the time being, just use a dummy file such as this one:

```
{
  "description" : "Test",
  "name" : "Perl 6 Quick Reference examples",
  "version" : "0.0.1"
}
```

Concluding Remarks

Testing is the most efficient way to check that your program is up to specifications and safe from underlying language or downstream libraries drift. Perl 6 includes Test as a core library and there are other libraries such as Test0 that you can use to test your programs; more libraries are specific to web or concurrent applications.

Besides knowing how to use Test and Test0, running these tests automatically and collecting their results is done through prove6; you can also configure Travis to run its tests for you via a YAML file. Most other continuous integration services run either the same file or a YAML file, so knowing its syntax will always help.

With tests, you are almost ready for preparing a whole module for release in the Perl 6 ecosystem. You'll see how to do this in the next chapter.

CHAPTER 14

Building Up a Project

How to Design and Create a Library to Release It to the Whole Wide World

Although there are always many ways to do anything in the Perl 6 world, if you want to release a distribution that includes several modules, test, and example scripts to the world, there are several conventions that will help standard installation commands such as zef do it correctly, and also so that other developers can navigate your source code should they wish to fork it for personal use or to improve it.

The most important thing in every project, however, is to document it. Perl 6 includes a mini-language for documenting its code. You'll see how it works next.

The examples in this chapter will be in their own repository. Sometimes they are too long to be included on the page, so it's better if you check them out on the Apress site (www.apress.com/ 9781484249550).

© J.J. Merelo 2019
J.J. Merelo, *Perl 6 Quick Syntax Reference*, https://doi.org/10.1007/978-1-4842-4956-7_14

Documenting Your Code with Pod6

Pod6 is kind of an acronym for plain old documentation, version 6. It is a domain-specific language that is used for commenting and adding textual information to code.

In most languages, comments are either inert or, if they use some specific format, interpreted by an external program. Pod6 is unique in the sense that it's an integral part of the language. Comments will be parsed and interpreted so that you can use the internal structure in the same way you use the grammar of a language.

The name Perl 6 uses for these mini-languages that are embedded into Perl 6 itself is *braids*. They include, besides documentation/comments, quoting and regular expressions.

In general, the documentation mini-language will be interpreted when

- Text is preceded by #. If it's followed by a letter, it will be interpreted as simple text that is not part of the documentation. If it's followed by another symbol, it will be include in the documentation.

- The first character in the line is = or the text is enclosed by block markers that use it. This is always part of the documentation, but its actual rendering will depend on the command.

This example includes both kinds of documentation:

```
unit class X::Cards::NoMore is Exception;

=begin pod
=head1 NAME
X::Cards::NoMore - Exception thrown when there are no more cards
```

```
=head1 SYNOPSIS
=for code
use X::Cards::NoMore;
throw X::Cards::NoMore;

=head1 DESCRIPTION
Thrown when there are no more cards in the deck.

=head1 METHODS
=end pod

#| Returns the exception message
method message() {
        "No more cards left, sorry";
}

=begin pod

=head1 AUTHOR
JJ Merelo <jjmerelo@gmail.com>

=head1 COPYRIGHT AND LICENSE
Copyright 2018,2019 JJ Merelo
This library is free software; you can redistribute it and/or
modify
it under the Artistic License 2.0.
=end pod
```

This code adds documentation to the X::Cards::NoMore exception class created in Chapter 11. This class has been chosen because it's the simplest class you have seen so far, but its documentation includes everything you need to know. Documentation is parsed by default, but in order to visualize it, you need to write

```
perl6 --doc lib/X/Cards/NoMore.pm6
```

This command will render the documentation as plain text, but it can also be used to render it in several other formats. These formats are available as modules in the ecosystem; see Table 14-1.

Table 14-1. *Main Pod conversion modules*

Pod renderer	Description
Pod::To::HTML	Produces HTML output
Pod::To::Markdown	Generates markdown files
Pod::To::Latex	Converts to the LaTeX document processing framework
Pod::To::Man	Generates a framework that can be processed by Unix's man

These modules get *plugged* in as soon as they are installed, so

```
perl6 --doc=HTML lib/X/Cards/NoMore.pm6
```

will render in HTML the standard output. In general, you will use -doc=XXX if the name of the installed module is Pod::To::XXX. By default it uses Pod::To::Text, which is included with the system.

Let's observe again the two kinds of documentation: prefixed with = for Pod commands, and prefixed with # for *smart* comments. The #| comment precedes a method declaration and will be rendered in the output along with the method signature. This way, it's easy to combine a markdown method such as Pod6 with comments in the generated documentation.

There are four types of Pod commands:

- **Block commands**: They use =begin and =end to indicate their span. For instance, pod blocks start with =begin pod and end with =end pod.

- **Paragraph commands**: They use =for and end in the first empty line, or use a standalone = command (like =head1). For instance, code can use =for code, with code starting in the next line.

- **Inline commands**: They use single letters and angular parenthesis for the code they are applied to. For instance, I<this> is used to italicize this.

- **Metadata**: They use ALL CAPS and how they are used is implementation-specific. For instance, =TITLE might be used to give the generated web page a title (and ignored if it's rendered in some other way).

In order to document your modules, the essential parts are shown in the example above. You can check out the documentation for the Deckie module in the same repository.

Parts of a Project and How to Build, Test, and Release It

Before creating the directory, you should maybe devote some time to giving an adequate name to it. If it's intended for the ecosystem, the single most important issue is to make sure that the chosen name has not been already used. It does not really matter if the subject is already in the ecosystem, since you might have a different approach or it might evolve in a different way.

And as a matter of fact, the Perl 6 ecosystem is able to support modules with the same name as long as the author, as expressed in the auth metadata field, is different. However, you should have a very good reason to do that.

Class and module names follow the extended syntax, with identifiers separated by double colons. These names are arbitrary, but in general the first identifier before the colon is a general field (like Math, or Test, or Web), followed by some specific name (Web::Cache, for instance). There might be more than two parts. A specific implementation of a web cache could be called Web::Cache::DB, for instance; exceptions generally are prefixed by X, and they have a second segment that is related to the class or field they are used in, like X::Cards, which is why the exception presented in Chapter 12 (and which you will use here) is called X::Cards::NoMore. These names will help everyone find your module. You can, however, opt for a simple and original name like the one you will be using here, Deckie.

In general, there are four groups of files included in a project:

- Source files

- Installable files, including scripts and/or documentation

- Metadata, which includes the module description, as well as other files such as the license and documentation

- Test files

Let's start with metadata, which is usually created with the repository if the repo hosting allows that. Several files are common to open source files hosted in a repository:

- **License**: This is a file that is usually called LICENSE and is in the main directory. The license is a write-up of all rights that are ceded to users of the software by the developer. There are many open source licenses, but the Perl world prefers the one called Artistic 2.0 license; it is included in the repo. A pointer to this license is

usually included in source files too; this is why in the
inline documentation for the module above there's a
reference to it.

- README.md **file**: A file with simple instructions to
  install the module and a small reference. One way to
  include a reference to the module methods generated
  automatically from Pod documentation is by using
  Pod::To::Markdown.

- .gitignore: This file includes patterns and globs that
  should generally be ignored by git. Besides whatever
  files are generated by your favorite editor, Perl 6
  generates a .precomp directory. Include that in a
  single line.

All of these files are convenient and conventionally used, but generic
for every kind of project. Metadata in a Perl 6 module is included in a JSON
file called META6.json and placed in the root directory, such as this one for
your module, which is simply called Deckie:

```
{
  "authors" : [ "JJ Merelo" ],
  "build-depends" : [ ],
  "depends" : [ ],
  "description" : "A card deck",
  "license" : "Artistic-2.0",
  "name" : "Deckie",
  "perl" : "6.*",
  "provides" : {
      "Deckie" : "lib/Deckie.pm6",
      "X::Cards::NoMore" : "lib/X/Cards/NoMore"
  },
```

```
"resources" : [ ],
"source-url" : "https://github.com/JJ/perl6-quick-reference-
chapter14.git",
"tags" : [ "apress", "games" ],
"test-depends" : [ ],
"version" : "0.0.1"
}
```

The usual key-value structure used in JSON files that act as configuration is respected here. It must be valid JSON, and there are a few keys that are mandatory. They are `name`, `description`, `provides`, and `perl`. The first two are used for naming and describing the module, and the last expresses the versions of Perl 6 this module works with. There are currently only two, 6.c and 6.d; 6.* means it will work with any.

The `provides` key includes an array with the name of the modules you will be including in the library, two in this case, and the files where you can find them.

The fact that you can enunciate these paths here shows that it's actually arbitrary where you place these files. In fact, it's customary to put them into a `lib` directory, with fragments of the name turned into subdirectories, as can be seen in the X::Cards::NoMore case.

The rest of the keys are not mandatory, but in the case of `source-url` and `version`, highly convenient. The installation program, zef, will use `version` to decide whether to install a new version, comparing it with the one that's already on your system. `Source-url` will be used to get to the place where it's been hosted, and it's usually a GitHub URL. `Depends`, `build-depends`, and `test-depends` are not used in this case, since this module does not depend on another one, but should include the module it needs to work (or to run the tests or to build it). The same goes for `license`, which should match the file you have included in the repo. This string follows the SPDX (software package data exchange) convention, which provides a unique way of identifying every license and is conventionally used in all modern languages. You can retrieve the whole list from `https://spdx.org/licenses/`.

This metadata file shows the conventions in the layout of directories in a Perl 6 module distribution. I have already shown which files are placed in the main directory. Besides them,

- Packages are placed in the `lib` directory, so that the module `X::Y::Z.pm6` is in the `lib/X/Y` directory.

- Examples and other files (such as data or documentation) are placed in the `resources` directory. These resources will be available to the library (and other) files via the `%?RESOURCES` hash You add them to the resources key this way:

  ```
  "resources" : [ "examples/deckie.p6" ],
  ```

  In this case, `%?RESOURCES<examples/deckie.p6>` will give you the location where that file is effectively installed.

- Executable files you want available need to be installed in the `bin/` directory; also, conventionally they have no extension. For instance, you save this file as `shuffle` and will be able to access from anywhere it once the module is installed:

  ```
  #!/usr/bin/env perl6
  use v6;
  use Deckie;
  say Deckie.new.draw( 40 ).join(" · " );
  ```

- Test files go to the `t/` directory, as indicated in Chapter 13. Additional tests (that need not be run every time), also called "author tests," are placed in the `xt/` directory.

How to test was explained extensively in Chapter 13. You will merge the tests seen there into a single file, but you need to add a new test for the module itself. This test

```
use Test;
use Test::META;
plan 1;
meta-ok;
```

will check that the META6.json file follows the correct syntax by running the meta-ok test. It will also check that it contains the mandatory fields, and that the formats for some fields (like license) are correct. Since tests are run in order, and this is one of the first things that should be checked, this test will be named 00-meta.t.

Test::META is not part of the standard distribution, so you will need to change the test-depends key to

```
"test-depends" : [ "Test::META" ],
```

This indicates that you will need that module only for testing, and it is not actually needed to make your library work permanently. Some module installation applications might choose to add it temporarily, or ask about it.

After all this, the module is ready to be tested. The same program, zef, that is used to install modules is also used to test your own, since passing tests is a requisite for them to be installed when downloaded or from source. Running

```
zef test .
```

will, in this case, run your two tests and yield something like

```
===> Testing: Deckie:ver<0.0.4>
===> Testing [OK] for Deckie:ver<0.0.4>
```

zef test . already takes care of adding -Ilib to the utility that is running the tests and will use any of the programs available. If prove (the Perl 5 version) is not installed, it will use a fallback internal TAP parser to compile the results of the tests.

It's convenient to run these tests automatically every time a push to master is made; they will also be run if some pull request is made to your module. As explained in Chapter 13, signing up for Travis (or other CI service) and adding a .travis.yml configuration file to your root directory is all you need. With every push or pull request, you will obtain a report that should be similar to Figure 14-1.

```
405  ===> Installing: Test::META.ver<0.0.10>:auth<github.jonathanstowe>:api<1.0>
406  ===> Testing: Deckie:ver<0.0.4>
407  ===> Testing [OK] for Deckie:ver<0.0.4>
408  The command "docker run -t -v $TRAVIS_BUILD_DIR:/test jjmerelo/test-perl6" exited with 0.
409
410
```

Figure 14-1. *Result of a Travis test for the module Deckie*

Finally, when everything is ready, you can publish it in the ecosystem, making it available (through zef) to all of the Perl 6 community. Almost half of Perl 6 users have, according to the latest survey, published one or more modules in the ecosystem, and the subjects Range from mathematics to glue to other programs such as git. If it's useful for you, it will probably be useful for someone else, and by publishing it you might get spontaneous collaboration.

Such as it is now, your library can already be used by anyone. Just download it and then run

zef install .

This will download all needed dependencies and make it available to all Perl 6 programs.

In general, Perl 6 is installed in userspace, which is why this step does not run in privileged mode. I strongly advise you to follow this practice; however, if you have installed your interpreter from some repository, you will have to run that as superuser (by prepending sudo or whatever mechanism your OS uses).

Obviously you might want to publish it in the ecosystem so that it can be found by name and downloaded as a dependence of any other library. There are two ways of doing this. One is by becoming a CPAN author and uploading a tar or zip file through an interface called PAUSE. However, there's the intermediate step of actually getting permissions from the CPAN cabal, so let's use the second method, which is simply called Perl 6 ecosystem. Do the following, step by step:

1. Get the *raw* URL of your `META6.json` as indicated in Figure 14-2 by right-clicking the button and selecting "get URL." This will look like `https://github.com/JJ/perl6-quick-reference-chapter14/raw/master/META6.json`, which is the repository name + `/raw/master/META6.json`.

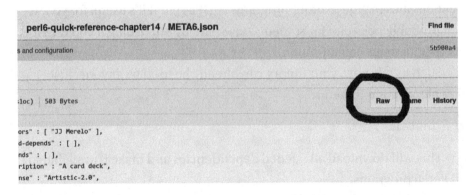

Figure 14-2. *Button with the raw URL of the META6.json file*

2. In order to add this to the ecosystem, you need to create a pull request on the ecosystem repo. Go to `https://github.com/perl6/ecosystem/blob/master/META.list` and click the pencil icon for editing. Add it anywhere you wish; it does not really matter.

3. When you've done so, use the subject "Add My::Module::Name to the ecosystem." No need to use a body. This will signal to people in charge of accepting pull requests (like me) that you want to add it to the ecosystem.

4. Select "**new branch** for this commit and start a pull request." This will create a pull request (ask us to *pull* this version of the file you've just created) and finally click "Propose file change."

That's basically it. Tests will be run on your `META6.json` file (but if you've followed advice above, you're good), plus some additional checks. Stick around for a while to see if there's some error, and fix it if that's the case; you'll need to add a comment to notify us that you've done something about it. If the tests pass, usually someone will accept the PR and your module will be available to the whole ecosystem. Still, changes need to be propagated to the ecosystem indices, but they are renovated every two hours, so inside of the next two hours you will be able to see your module. Type

```
zef search My::Awesome::Module
```

and it will show up there. When that happens, announce it to the whole wide world! Your contribution to the community will be much appreciated.

Concluding Remarks

This chapter has been a quick reference of the commands, configuration files, and conventions involved in publishing a module to the Perl 6 ecosystem. If you browse the ecosystem, you will see that they go from the whimsical to the mission critical, so feel free to add to them.

In the next chapter, you will learn how to analyze semi-structured text using one of Perl 6's most powerful tools: grammars. On your way to grammars you will work with regular expressions, which are the building blocks.

CHAPTER 15

Grammars

One of the Features That Makes Perl 6 Unique, and One of the Most Powerful Ways of Processing Text

Opening a file or group of files, extracting information from them from its regular structure, and performing additional operations are quintessential scripting tasks. Regular expressions are present in every modern language and will help you match the structure in a string (considering a document as a very long string sometimes). Perl 6 takes the concept a bit further: grammars collect regular expressions and can be applied to complex constructions such as protocols or even programming languages.

The syntax of regexes (sometimes called *regexen*) is common to many languages, although Perl 6 adapts it to its Unicode features and throws other goodies in. You'll see this next.

Processing Text Using Regular Expressions

Regular expressions are objects in Perl 6, but in the same way as other native objects, they can be created using literals:

```
say /foo/.^name; # Regex
```

J.J. Merelo, *Perl 6 Quick Syntax Reference*, https://doi.org/10.1007/978-1-4842-4956-7_15

The // syntax declares a regex literal, which in this case would match any string that included, anywhere, the letters f, o, o in that exact sequence. This can also be expressed using the quoting construct rx

```
say rx/foo/.^name;
say rx«foo».^name;
```

in which case, as shown, any paired set of quotes or braces/brackets can be used for legibility.

Additionally, the syntax m// does not create an object; it is used instead to directly evaluate if the topic variable, or the variable it's smartmatched with, matches the regular expression,

```
for <foo bar baz> {
    say "$_ matches" if m/foo/;
}
```

which is totally equivalent to

```
for <foo bar baz> -> $m {
    say "$m matches" if $m ~~ m/foo/;
}
```

Smartmatch will return a Bool if there's no match; however, it will return a Match object if there's actually a match. As shown above, a Match object will be Boolified to True. Regular expressions and grammars are actually a very integral part of Perl 6, so the results of successful matches also get their own special variable, $/, which stores the Match object resulting from the last regex even if it hasn't been stored anywhere. You can obviously store it in a variable:

```
for <foo bar baz> -> $m {
    my $match = $m ~~ m/foo/;
    say $match.perl;
}
```

This will print

```
Match.new(pos => 3, made => Any, from => 0, hash => Map.
new(()), orig => "foo", list => ())
```

followed by two Bool::False, showing the internal structure of Match objects, which are quite powerful. They are Captures, which means that they will offer a Positional as well as Associative interface to the results of the match. See Table 15-1.

Table 15-1. *Match attributes*

Method	Description
pos	Last cursor position while matching
from, to	Character that starts and finishes the match
orig	Original object matched
prematch, postmatch	Strings in front of and behind the match

However, regular expressions are much more powerful that just checking if a string is included in another. As in other cases (Positionals, for instance), their matching behavior can be modified by adverbs. Table 15-2 shows some of the adverbs you can use in match expressions.

Table 15-2. *Selected adverbs used in match expressions*

Adverb	Description
nth (list of positions)	Matches only if they are in the indicated positions.
1st, 2nd, 3rd	Matches the first, second, or third appearance of the string.
g, global	Captures all matches, not only the first one.
pos (position)	The match should occur in a particular position.

For instance, here

```
my $match = "stafoostatic" ~~ m:g:2nd/sta/;
say "From {$match.prematch} to {$match.postmatch}";
```

you use two adverbs, one to take into account all matches, not just the first one, :g, but then you indicate through the :2nd adverb (which is actually equivalent to :nd(2)) that the match you're interested in is the second. This will print

```
From stafoo to tic
```

showing that, effectively, it's the second sta the one that's matched. Please note that you can use adverbs in any order.

You can only go so far by matching single strings. Regexes, however, are a whole language to express their structure. These directives are related to text repetitions. See Table 15-3.

Table 15-3. *Quantifiers and other regex symbols*

Directives	Description
.	Stands for any character.
?	Postfix indicating it can appear or not.
*	Postfix for "will appear a number of times, or maybe not."
+	Postfix for "will appear for sure, maybe many times."
" "	Quoting will again mean the actual string, including whitespace and symbols, since spaces are meaningless in regexes (unless indicated otherwise).

Let's see how this work in practice:

```
say "foo baz bar" ~~ m/ fo+" ba".?" ba"r* /; # 「foo baz bar」
```

This regex starts to show the power, but also, of course, what has made regexes infamous. At first sight, they look like line noise; but in fact, with just a few directives you are now able to work with a wide Range of string structures. Perl 6 adds non-significant whitespace for clarity, which in this case allows you to separate the slashes from the beginning and end of the actual regex. The rest of the quantifiers above are used in this expression, even together: . ? simply indicates that there can be, or not, a single character following the literal " ba" (with a preceding space). The result is surrounded by the Japanese-style quotes by choice, since this is how the .gist method acts in the case of a Match.

Another group of symbols allows you to match alternatives or conjunctions, also to make matching stop and not be greedy. See Table 15-4.

Table 15-4. *Alternatives, frugal quantifier and expression joiners*

Symbol	Description
?	Frugal quantifier; following * or + will stop in the first character that makes something true.
[]	Groups alternatives or sets of regexes visually or syntactically.
|	Expresses alternatives. Will match the first that's true.
||, <>	Longest alternative: will match the longest. Expressions between quotes will behave as this operator.
&, &&	Joins expressions that must be matched by the same string (or fragment).

In these examples,

```
say "foo baz bar" ~~ m:g/ [fo+ | ba.] /; # (⌈foo⌋ ⌈baz⌋ ⌈bar⌋)
say "foo bar baz" ~~ m/ fo.+?b /; # ⌈foo b⌋
say "10 ♥" ~~ m/ ..? " " "♥" | "♠" | "♣" | "♦" /; # ⌈10 ♥⌋
```

you use some of them. Please note that the enclosing square brackets are used in the first, but omitted in the last one. If the second match was not frugal, it would have matched greedily "foo bar b".

Most times, however, you are not so much interested in matching but in extracting a particular part of the string. You will need to indicate your intent in the regex via parentheses:

```
my $card =  "10 ♥" ~~ m/ (..?) " " ("♥" | "♠" | "♣" | "♦") /;
say $card;
.say for $card.list;
```

In this case, your successful match has been assigned to a Math variable. However, this Match is going to contain much more information that what it did before, since it will effectively host the results of the matching operation; when getting the gist of it via say, it will print the matched string as well as every one of the single captures. This lists of captures is available also via the .list method; and every one of these captures will also be a Match, as shown by the funky way of printing them.

Remember the special Match variable $/? This one will also host the result and will make it available as a list, so that say $/[0] will print the first capture. Additionally, these captures will create a set of special variables starting with $0. $0, again, will print the same result.

When there are many captures, however, it might be better to name them, so that they can be referred by name and not by order. This is why Match acts as a Capture, to leverage its Positional and Associative qualities.

```
my $card =  "10 ♥"
    ~~ m/ $<value> = (..?) " "   $<suit> = ("♥" | "♠" | "♣" |
"♦")  /;
say $_.key => $_.value for $card.hash;
say "$<value> of $<suit>";
```

Named captures have their own syntax, which includes angular braces; they are directly inserted into the regex, preceding the sub-regex that is going to be captured. While the Positional captures will be available in Match.list, these are going to be available from Match.hash. But remember that $card is a Match and thus a Capture, so captured strings are going to be available by name: $card<value> or $/<suit>, for instance.

There are some patterns that are repeated often, or even kinds of characters that are often grouped. Regexes also include an escaped letter to represent groups of letters. Table 15-5 shows a few.

Table 15-5. *Escaped character classes*

Character classes	Description
\s, \S	Whitespace, and whatever is not whitespace.
\d, \D	Digit and the opposite.
\w, \W	Characters you can find in a word, and the opposite. Alphanumeric characters are considered a "word."
\t, \T, \v, \V, \n, \N, \h, \H	Tab characters, vertical spaces, carriage returns, horizontal whitespaces (and the opposite).

Let's rewrite the previous expression using these character classes:

```
say  "3 ♣" ~~ / (\d+) \s+  (\W)  /;
```

It's much clearer now, and besides, it's much more precise than it was. In regular expressions, you need to not only match and extract the correct substrings, but also avoid false positives. In this case, it will avoid matching things like "AA ♣". However, there's now a new imprecision: \W will match any single character that's not alphanumeric. You can express character classes much more precisely using Unicode character properties, which use the <:property> syntax. They come in two flavors: character properties and categories. Character properties refer to the type of script and the block, two broad categories that can be used to check for alphabets. You could substitute \W with <:Block('Miscellaneous Symbols')>. That's not earning you much, since it's actually longer than enumerating the four suits. Using <:So> (for Other_Symbol general category) will be shorter, but still there are many more symbols in that category. Eventually, you settle for

```
say  "10 ♦" ~~ / (\d+) \s+ (<[♥ ♠ ♣ ♦]>)  /;
```

The <[ ]> allows you to directly include character categories; as usual, whitespace is not taken into account. Any character literal can be used, including \x and \c specifications, and you can even use *arithmetic* to add or subtract categories. For instance, this will include all numbers except Latin ones:

```
my $non-latin-digits = rx/  <[\d] - [0..9]>+  /;
for  <ハ  33> {
    say $_ ~~ $non-latin-digits;
}
```

This will print ⌈ハ⌋ the first iteration, but Nil in the second, since the two Latin digits will not match the expression. Please note also that you have reused an expression via the quoting construct rx. The categories with which you are doing arithmetic are both in square brackets. The – is used in the same sense as in a numerical expression: all digits (of all alphabets) excluding or minus the 10 Latin digits. The whole construct gets a + at the end, indicating that it might appear once or several times.

The last function of a regular expression is to replace part of a string, a data munging operation that is very frequently carried out by scripting languages such as Perl 6. Substitution uses s as a command and this syntax:

```
$_ = "A ♥,A ♣";
s/","/█/;
.say;
```

This just substitutes the comma for a block character. Since strings are immutable (they're literals), the s command needs to act on variables. You just alias the string to the topic variable, and s, by default, will act on it. .say will also be applied as a method to the topic variable, so that will print A ♥█A ♣.

So far you have been using whitespace as separator, but there are many different ways of ending a word; words are delimited in many possible ways (punctuation, for instance) but sometimes you are only interested in knowing where a word starts or ends. Regex can take care of that too, with the *boundary operators* shown in Table 15-6.

Table 15-6. *Boundary operators*

Boundary operator	Description
`<|w>`, `<?wb>`, `<!wb>`	Any word boundary; (last) not a word boundary.
`<<`, `«`, `>>`, `»`	Left and right word boundary.
`^`, `$`	Start, end of string.
`^^`, `$$`	Start, end of line.

You can use these operators in match, extraction, and substitution operations:

```
$_ = "3♠";
s/^«(.+)»(<[♥ ♠ ♣ ♦]>)$/$1$0/;
.say;
```

If you want to extract part of the match to use for substitution, the same syntax mentioned before for captures is used. In this case, you capture a few characters that form a word at the beginning of a string `^«(.+)»` together with a suit symbol at the end of a string (`<[♥♠♣♦]>)$`; you invert them putting the latter before the former. This will print ♠3.

Regexes are code, but they can also trigger code when a match is produced. Insert a block behind a statement, and it will be run every time it's matched:

```
"<zipi><zape>" ~~ m:g/ '<' ~ '>' (\w+) { say $/[0] } /;
```

You can see a new syntax for enclosed strings here, which uses the tilde (~) between the two symbols that will be used for enclosing strings, in this case angular brackets. The actual regex that will be matched is *behind* this expression; since you also want to capture, you write (\w+). Right behind that, you open the block that will get the whole string to match as a topic variable, but also the match in the usual $/. Since within the match itself the captured string will be the first one, $/[0] will contain what's just been matched, and this will print

```
⌈zipi⌋
⌈zape⌋
```

Regexen as Functions

Perl 6 is a functional language. This means that functions are first class objects, but it might also mean that what we think of as pieces of static data, or complex data structures, are actually functions too and can behave as such. Case in point: regexes are actually functions.

```
my $r = rx/foo/;
say $r.^mro
```

will print

```
((Regex) (Method) (Routine) (Block) (Code) (Any) (Mu))
```

Which, surprisingly, makes a Regex a Method, and thus a Callable. For the time being, this type of callable has no arguments, but it is going to be called if you use it in a smartmatch (as you have seen), or if you include it in another expression:

```
my $suits = rx/<[♥ ♠ ♣ ♦]>/;
say "Q♠" ~~ /^«(.+)»($suits)$/;
```

```
# ⌈Q♠⌋
# 0 => ⌈Q⌋
# 1 => ⌈♠⌋
```

By simply inserting the name of the regex inside another regex, it's *called*, acting as if what it represents is actually there.

This way of representing a regex is akin to declaring a block on the fly. But routines have another formal way of declaring them, directly, giving them a name: sub, method or, in this case, also regex:

```
my regex suits { <[♥ ♠ ♣ ♦]> };
say "Q♠" ~~ /^«(.+)»<suits>$/;
# ⌈Q♠⌋
# 0 => ⌈Q⌋
# suits => ⌈♠⌋
```

The syntax is very similar to declaring them as (let's call them) "block"-regex. But you're using regex syntax inside the curly braces that delimit the regex code.

Also, you declare them with lexical scope with my. Not doing that will give a somewhat cryptic error along the lines of not being a suitable declaration for a method, so you use my (or our, if you're declaring it with package scope). You're also using a special syntax for including the regex as a sub-regex inside the other. <> has been used extensively within regexes, mostly with another sigil. If you use them this way, it will assume that the identifier it encloses is another regex and will include it right there. You can use this routine-like regex also by itself, but since you'll be using it as an object and not *calling* it, you'll slap the & sigil in front:

```
say "♣ ♦" ~~ &suits; # ⌈♣⌋
```

Since it's routine, can you call it as such? Curiously enough, you can. But remember, it's a method, and you need to call methods on objects, or else use whatever they are going to use as self as an argument. What will a regex use as self? Unsurprisingly, $/ or any Match object. If you call it right after the statement above, you'll get

```
say suits( $/ ); # ⌜♦⌟
```

That is, it continues checking on the string above right where it left it and returns the next match. This is why the Match object stores the position where the last search left off, to pick it up again right where it started.

Some of these regex-as-methods are predefined, and include usual patterns. Some of them are shown in Table 15-7.

Table 15-7. *Main character classes*

Character class	Description
<punct>	Punctuation and symbols that are not included in ASCII
<graph>	<alnum> (\w) and <punct>
<same>	Matches only between two identical characters
<print>	<graph> and \s (a.k.a. <space>)
<ident>	Matches a Perl 6 identifier
<xdigit>	Hexa digit
<upper>, <lower>	Uppercase and lowercase characters

Regexes use a mechanism called backtracking, which basically means that they interpret the regex from left to right, scanning the string and trying to match as much as possible every regex operator. Once they're done with an operator, they proceed to the next, but if that new operator introduces a new possible match, they *backtrack*, shedding some characters from the first one and matching them with the second one. You can see this in the operation in the following example that builds a regex piecemeal:

```
$_ = "foostastic";

say m/(\w+)/;
# ⌈foostastic⌋
# 0 => ⌈foostastic⌋
say m/(\w+)s/;
# ⌈foostas⌋
# 0 => ⌈foosta⌋
say m/(\w+) s \w ** 4 /;
# ⌈foostast⌋
# 0 => ⌈foo⌋
```

The third expression, which is the most complete, will actually work step by step as shown.

This code also introduces the *quantifier* operator, ∗∗, which indicates that the preceding expression will happen a certain number of times or a Range.

So it will first find the \w+ part and will greedily swallow the whole string, as shown in the first step. But then it will proceed to the second part of the regex, which includes an s. It will *backtrack* to the first s that's there, the one before tic. But then, as it proceeds to the third term in the expression, it will realize that once again it took too much and will backtrack again, matching just foo.

As you can imagine, this process is expensive, even more so with complicated regexes and long strings, since it might need to backtrack multiple times, ending up running over the strings many more times that needed. That is why Perl 6 introduces tokens: tokens are regular expressions that do not backtrack. Once they match something, it remains matched:

```
my token any-letter        { <alpha>+ }
my token any-letter-plus-s { <alpha>+ s }
say "foostastic" ~~ &any-letter;
say "foostastic" ~~ &any-letter-plus-s;
```

The first token will match the string, but not the second, because it will gobble up the whole string, and will have no s beyond that to match. The second smartmatch will print Nil.

Tokens can be used in the same way as regexes above, installed within other regexes (or tokens). They will also capture to a Match key of the same name, but you can change the name of the key using this syntax:

```
my token any-letter { <alpha>+ }

say "foo,bar" ~~ m/<first=any-letter><punct><second=any-letter>/;
```

You are using a token just like any other regex; the regex itself will backtrack, but that part will not, although in this particular case a regex would behave in the same way. The output in this case will be rather verbose:

```
⌜foo,bar⌟
 any-letter => ⌜foo⌟
  alpha => ⌜f⌟
  alpha => ⌜o⌟
  alpha => ⌜o⌟
```

```
first => ⌈foo⌋
 alpha => ⌈f⌋
 alpha => ⌈o⌋
 alpha => ⌈o⌋
punct => ⌈,⌋
any-letter => ⌈bar⌋
 alpha => ⌈b⌋
 alpha => ⌈a⌋
 alpha => ⌈r⌋
second => ⌈bar⌋
 alpha => ⌈b⌋
 alpha => ⌈a⌋
 alpha => ⌈r⌋
```

But it's interesting to render it in full to show the recursive nature of this regex. Since every routine-syntax character class will capture, it will generate matches at three levels: at the top level, at the any-letter (and punct) level, and at the lower level, <alpha>, since that character class is used from any-letter. This looks like a parsing tree, and indeed it's something like one, but already it shows how Perl 6 regexes have this power of decomposing a string into the structures described in it. Besides, there are keys *both* for the any-letter *and* the name you have given it, first and second. However, having these aliases allow you to use them directly, for instance printing $<second> or using them in a substitution. Or extracting them as tokens.

The third type of *functional* regex, rule, is a token in which space is significant. This can be enabled in a regex using the :sigspace adverb, but is so common that it gets its own name:

```
my token word { <alpha>+ }
my rule comma-separated {<word><punct> <word>}
say "foo, bar" ~~ &comma-separated;
```

The word token is used to build up the comma-separated rule, which is then used to parse a string. The result will be as expected, a match that will extract the two words keyed to word, akin to extracting two tokens in a programming language. Which is precisely why they are called tokens.

But this rule has been built using already defined regexes in the same lexical scope, and you are using it to parse a string, as if it were a grammar. You can do this more systematically in the grammars that you will see next.

Building Up Text Processors Using Grammars

Grammars are parsers that include several interdependent regexes in the same lexical scope. In the same way that methods are composed into classes, regexes (which are methods, and include tokens and rules) are composed into grammars to create a single, complex, and stateful way of processing a string. Grammars are declared in a similar way to classes (which is what they are):

```
grammar Game {
    token TOP { <player>  \s+ <action> \s+ <card> }
    token card    { [ <[1..9]> | "10" | <[AJQK]> ] ["♥" | "♠" |
    "♣" | "♦"] }
    token action { <alpha>+ }
    token player { <upper><alpha>+ }
}

say Game.parse( "Alice plays K♠");
```

Game.parse will return a Match, and it will look like this:

```
⌈Alice plays K♠⌋
 player => ⌈Alice⌋
  upper => ⌈A⌋
  alpha => ⌈l⌋
  alpha => ⌈i⌋
  alpha => ⌈c⌋
  alpha => ⌈e⌋
 action => ⌈plays⌋
  alpha => ⌈p⌋
  alpha => ⌈l⌋
  alpha => ⌈a⌋
  alpha => ⌈y⌋
  alpha => ⌈s⌋
  card => ⌈K♠⌋
```

Grammars are declared using the keyword grammar, and since they are classes, they conventionally use caps in the declaration. They consist of a series of regexes, which are their methods, out of which the most important one is the TOP, which is the regex the submitted string will be matched to.

Since tokens are more efficient than regex functions when processing strings (because they don't backtrack), traditionally grammars are populated with tokens and rules (which are also regex-as-methods), but you can also use regexes if you want or your grammar needs it. In this case, you don't need to use the scope declarator my since, effectively, these tokens get an implicit "has" as part of the Game class.

Grammars have, besides parse, two other methods: parsefile and subparse. The latter is used to apply a grammar to part of a string, not the whole one:

```
grammar G {
    token TOP { <alpha>+ }
}

say G.parse( "abcd" );
say G.parse( "abcd3" );
say G.subparse( "abcd3" );

constant filename = "/tmp/letters.txt";
spurt( filename, "foostastic");
say G.parsefile( filename );
unlink filename;
```

This is a simple grammar, with just one token. It needs to parse a whole string, as shown in the first sentence. The second one will fail, but it will work using subparse. The second block shows how the parsefile method works directly on a file, matching its content.

Since grammars are classes and tokens are methods, you should be able to parameterize them and use them in the same way any other class would.

The main difference is that you will be using only *class*, not *instance* methods. Grammars as classes will never be instantiated.

So you can put them in their own file, using unit as declaration. Call it Game.pm6.

```
unit grammar Game;
token TOP ($separator) { <hand>+ % $separator }
```

```
token hand { <player>  \s+ <action> \s+ <card> }
token card    { [ <[1..9]> | "10" | <[AJQK]> ] ["♥" | "♠" | "♣"
| "♦"] }
token action { <alpha>+ }
token player { <upper><alpha>+ }
```

It's an evolution of the previous grammar, but you have added another
token at the top that parses game actions separated by a separator, to be
defined. You can use it from any script this way:

```
use Game;


my $game-desc1 = "Alice plays 7♥,Bob plays 8♠";
say Game.parse( $game-desc1, :args(( ",",)) );
$game-desc1 ~~ s/","/|/;
say Game.parse( $game-desc1, :args(( "|",)) );
```

The first sentence is the string you want to parse. While you have called
before parse with the string as argument, you need to tell it now what the
arguments for TOP are going to be. They are necessarily a list, which is
why you add , to ",", which creates an one-element list, and handles it to the
named argument args. This argument will be bound to $separator within
the grammar.

You use a substitution to give the string another separator and call the
grammar again with this new separator. The result will in both cases be the
same: there will be a match. You can print it directly as above, or render it
this way:

```
my $match = Game.parse( $game-desc1, :args(( "|",)) );
for $match<hand>.list -> $hand {
    say "Playing→ $hand";
}
```

Every grammar token will get a key in the Match object, and you will be able to get the list of them using the Match as a hash (a Capture, actually). This will print

```
Playing→ Alice plays 7♥
Playing→ Bob plays 8♠
```

Perl 6's other mechanisms, such as multiple schedule, come in handy in grammars too. They are used to make different strings trigger the same token. You use one in this module, called Cards.pm6:

```
token TOP ($separator = ",") { <hand>+ % $separator }
token hand { <player>  \s+ <action> \s+ <card> }
token card    { [ <[1..9]> | "10" | <[AJQK]> ] ["♥" | "♠" | "♣"
| "♦"] }
proto token action {*}
token action:sym<plays> { <sym> }
token action:sym<draws> { <sym> }
token action:sym<wins> { <sym> }
token player { <upper><alpha>+ }
```

It's similar to the previous one, except you have used multiple schedule for action and also given $separator a default value, so that you don't have to invoke it with args every time.

You need to declare first the name of the token via proto, as usual. But then, instead of using the same name and different signatures for identifying which code is going to be called, grammars use :sym<string> for selecting the specific token that is going to be used; that string is represented by <sym> inside the multi. So the first action will trigger when "plays" is found, the second when "draws" is found, and there's also <*>, which will trigger in any other case. Using it this way,

```
my $match = Cards.parse( "Alice plays 7♥,Bob draws 8♠,
Cara wins A♦" );
for $match<hand> -> $h {
    say "Action→ $h<action>";
}
```

you will extract, for every hand, the action part, which will be printed.

Tokens can be used independently, which is useful when you want to debug them separately:

Assume use `Cards`; from now on if the `Cards` class is used in the program.

```
say Cards.parse( "Alice plays 7♥", :rule<hand> );
say Cards.parse( "wins", :rule<action> );
```

Remember that rule, token, and regex are sometimes used interchangeably here. Even if the grammar is composed of tokens (as is the case) or even regexes, I will refer to them by rule in this context. In the first case, the hand token is going to be applied to the string; in the second case, it will be the multi token `action`. Grammars are then shown to be, among other things, a collection of regular expressions you can also use for checking sub-strings or standalone.

The true power of grammars comes from the fact that, besides checking and parsing complex structures, you can take actions depending on what has been matched. In the case of a programming language, that action would be running the statement; in other cases, it would be interpreting the parsed document and creating another one. Possible actions are only bound by the language itself. Classes bound to grammars are called actions, and they are simply classes that include methods for tokens in the original grammar.

This is one of the simplest grammar actions:

```
unit class Cards-Action;
method TOP ($/) { make ~$/ }
```

All methods in grammar actions will have $/ as an argument, the match object. You can use any other argument, but it will behave in a slightly different way, the only difference being that you can no longer use make as a subroutine, since in that form it acts directly on $/:

```
method TOP ($match) { $match.make: ~$match }
```

What you are going to do is just print the match if it's correct; this will be contained in $/ and you will stringify it by preceding it with ~. But the important part is the make command. This command will effectively *produce* the output, inserting it into the production attribute of the match. The rest of the tokens are processed by default, that is, they simply produce a $/ that will be passed on to the next level.

You can use this action now this way:

```
use Cards;
use Cards-Action;
my $to-parse = "Alice plays 7♥,Bob draws 8♠,Cara wins A♦";
my $match = Cards.parse( $to-parse, actions => Cards-Action.new
);
say $match.made;
```

The $match variable will contain your regular match; but calling the .made method will return what was produced by the grammar actions. In this case, it will simply reprint the string that was matched successfully. In general, make will produce a string that can be retrieved at a higher level using .made.

You can (and should) create actions for every single token. This will allow you to disregard some of them if needed. For instance,

```
unit class Cards-Who;
method TOP ($/) { make join("", $/<hand>».made ) }
method hand( $/ ) {
    make ~$/<player> ~ ' → ' ~ ~$/.<card> ~ "\n"
}
```

which, when used from this script,

```
my $to-parse = "Alice plays 7♥,Bob draws 8♠,Cara wins A♦";
my $match = Cards.parse( $to-parse,
                         actions => Cards-Who );
say $match.made;
```

will print

```
Alice → 7♥
Bob → 8♠
Cara → A♦
```

You read the grammar actions from bottom to TOP, since this is the way the string is parsed. You have only provided actions for hand and TOP, but this is enough to produce a report from the initial string without much code.

The hand action is relatively straightforward. You stringify the result of the player and card that are part of every hand and add a bit of formatting so that they are printed one to a line. But you use make to add that production to every hand match, that is, every match will now contain, besides their usual fields, a production that will be that string the hand has been reduced to.

Stepping up to TOP, that match will contain everything that's been matched below, including a list of matches for hand. But now, every element of the list will contain what has been produced in the previous actions. `$/<hand>».made` will call `.made` on every element of the via the `>>` operator. You join the resulting lines and call `make` to make that production hitch on the match it returns.

The only change you have made to the script is that you're calling actions with the class, not an instance. It's actually doesn't matter that you use one or the other in this case, since that class does not really have any instance variables. With them, there will obviously be a difference.

Concluding Remarks

Regexes and their mothers, grammars, are incredibly powerful mechanisms that actually embed a specific language within Perl 6, giving it the feature of being able to process semi-structured documents and, from them, actually produce new strings or any activity you describe within them. Besides, they are integrated nicely within the whole Perl 6 concept: regex are routines, grammars are classes. As such, they are first class citizens and can be integrated modularly into big applications. Besides, grammars are published in the ecosystem in the same way any other module or class is, with distributions such as Grammar::Common including a lot of useful functionality. Besides, what this distribution actually includes are roles, which can be easily mixed in your own grammars, saving you the work of writing your own grammars for simple things like infix or prefix expressions.

Grammars have often being called the killer feature of Perl 6. This might be the case (along with its full support of Unicode), but what they really are is the crucible of Perl 6, since most of the concepts that make it unique, from roles to regular expressions, are put to work in them. This is why they were left for the last chapter of the book.

The next chapter will have to be written by you, using all the resources available for Perl 6 users, including its wonderful community, to which you will be heartily welcome.

Index

Printed in the United States
By Bookmasters